S K HAMPSHIRE

AI FOR BEGINNERS

UNLOCKING THE FUTURE: A SIMPLE GUIDE TO UNDERSTANDING AND USING ARTIFICIAL INTELLIGENCE

Copyright © 2024 by S K Hampshire

All rights reserved. No part of this publication may be reproduced, stored or transmitted in any form or by any means, electronic, mechanical, photocopying, recording, scanning, or otherwise without written permission from the publisher. It is illegal to copy this book, post it to a website, or distribute it by any other means without permission.

S K Hampshire asserts the moral right to be identified as the author of this work.

S K Hampshire has no responsibility for the persistence or accuracy of URLs for external or third-party Internet Websites referred to in this publication and does not guarantee that any content on such Websites is, or will remain, accurate or appropriate.

Designations used by companies to distinguish their products are often claimed as trademarks. All brand names and product names used in this book and on its cover are trade names, service marks, trademarks and registered trademarks of their respective owners. The publishers and the book are not associated with any product or vendor mentioned in this book. None of the companies referenced within the book have endorsed the book.

First edition

This book was professionally typeset on Reedsy.
Find out more at reedsy.com

Contents

Introduction	1
Purpose of the Book: Why AI Matters to You	1
Who This Book Is For: Beginners and Professionals	3
How to Make the Most of This Guide:	3
Chapter 1: Understanding AI Fundamentals	5
AI 101: The Basics and Definitions	5
Types of AI: What's the Difference?	6
Busting Common Myths	7
AI in Your Daily Life	8
Chapter 2: How AI Works	10
Core Components Made Simple	10
Neural Networks Unplugged	12
Different Learning Styles in AI	13
Chapter 3: Practical Applications for Everyday Use	18
Using AI in Personal Life, Entertainment, and Leisure	18
AI for Health and Wellness	21
AI Revolutionizing Businesses and Creative Industries	24
Chapter 4: Overcoming Common Struggles	28
Navigating Terminology and Concepts	28
Translating Theory into Practice	33
Best Practices for Using AI Tools	36
Chapter 5: Getting Started with AI Tools	38
Essential AI Tools and Platforms	38
Kickstarting Your First AI Project	39
Step-by-Step Adventure Guide	42
Essential Resources and Datasets	44

Prompt Writing Hacks: Crafting the Perfect Input	49
Chapter 6: Understanding the Importance of Data	58
Data: The Heartbeat of AI	58
Collecting and Prepping Your Data	60
Understanding AI Ethics and Bias: Your Responsibility	61
Chapter 7: Empowerment for the Future	63
Exciting Trends and Innovations on the Horizon	63
Challenges and Responsibilities Ahead	64
Imagining a World with AI	65
Chapter 8: Your AI Journey Starts Here!	67
Setting Your Personal AI Goals	67
Building Your Community and Networking	68
Staying Ahead of the Curve	69
Chapter 9: Learning Resources for AI Adventurers	72
Books and Articles to Fuel Your Curiosity	72
Articles and Blogs	72
Further Reading and Exploration	74
Online Courses: Your AI Academy	75
Conclusion: Embrace Your AI Future!	79
Recap of Key Takeaways	79
Words of Encouragement for Ongoing Exploration	80
Final Thoughts: AI and You	81
GLOSSARY OF TERMS	84
References	88

Introduction

Welcome to the World of AI! Artificial Intelligence (AI) is no longer just a concept confined to science fiction. It's a part of our daily lives, influencing how we communicate, work, and even think. As you embark on this journey through "AI for Beginners: Unlocking the Future," you'll discover not only the fundamentals of AI but also how to harness its potential in practical ways.

Purpose of the Book: Why AI Matters to You

Understanding the Significance of AI in Daily Life: From the moment you wake up to your smart alarm to the time you wind down with a streaming service suggesting your next favorite show, AI is seamlessly integrated into your routine. This chapter will elucidate how AI impacts your life, making tasks easier, more efficient, and often more enjoyable.

Empowerment Through Knowledge: The more you understand AI, the better equipped you are to make informed decisions—whether it's choosing the right tools for work or simply navigating the tech landscape. Knowledge is power, and this book is designed to empower you to take control of your AI journey.

Understanding AI in Everyday Life

Everyday Applications of AI

Smart Assistants: Explore how devices like Siri, Alexa, and Google Assistant simplify daily tasks—setting reminders, answering questions, and controlling smart home devices. These examples illustrate how AI serves as an extension of our capabilities.

Personalized Experiences: Discuss AI's role in personalizing online experiences, such as tailored shopping recommendations on platforms like Amazon or curated playlists on Spotify, showcasing its capability to adapt to individual preferences.

The Transformative Nature of AI

Enhancing Productivity: AI tools can automate routine tasks, freeing up time for more complex and creative endeavors. From scheduling appointments to managing emails, understanding these tools can significantly boost productivity.

Problem Solving: Highlight how AI aids in problem-solving across various sectors — be it in healthcare with diagnostic algorithms or in finance with fraud detection systems. These real-world applications demonstrate AI's practical significance.

Empowering Readers with Knowledge

Breaking Down Barriers

Approachable Language: Throughout this book, we will simplify complex jargon, making AI concepts accessible to all. Our goal is to remove the intimidation factor associated with AI, showing you that it's not just for tech experts but for everyone.

Cultivating Curiosity: We encourage you to ask questions and engage with the content actively. Your journey through AI is personal, and curiosity will guide you toward deeper understanding and insight.

Engaging with the Material

Hands-On Learning: This book includes exercises and examples that encourage you to apply what you learn. Engaging with practical applications reinforces understanding and retention.

Reflection and Application: After each chapter, take a moment to reflect on how the information applies to your life. Whether you're contemplating a new project at work or considering how AI can streamline your daily tasks, active engagement is key.

Who This Book Is For: Beginners and Professionals

Beginners Curious About AI

Starting from Scratch: If you're new to AI, this book serves as a friendly guide, breaking down concepts into digestible pieces. Each chapter builds upon the last, ensuring a smooth learning curve.

Confidence Building: We aim to instill confidence in your ability to understand and use AI. With clear explanations and relatable examples, you'll find that AI is not as daunting as it seems.

Professionals Seeking Practical Applications

Leveraging AI in the Workplace: For those already familiar with the basics, this book offers insights into how AI can be applied in various industries. Discover tools that enhance efficiency, data analysis, and decision-making.

Innovating and Adapting: As industries evolve, so must professionals. This book helps you stay ahead of the curve, exploring emerging trends and practical applications of AI in your field.

How to Make the Most of This Guide:

Reading Order and Engaging with Examples

Navigating the Chapters: While each chapter is structured to stand alone, we recommend following the sequence for a cohesive understanding of AI. Each chapter builds on the concepts introduced in the previous ones, creating a comprehensive learning experience.

Finding Your Focus: Feel free to skim through sections that may seem familiar, but don't skip the exercises and examples — these are designed to reinforce your learning and enhance your practical understanding.

Engaging with Examples

Real-World Scenarios: Throughout the book, we will present real-world examples that illustrate AI applications, making the concepts relatable and easier to grasp.

Reflection Points: After each chapter, take time to reflect on what you've learned and how it applies to your life. Consider journaling your thoughts or discussing them with peers to deepen your understanding.

Summary

As we venture into the fascinating world of AI, remember that this journey is not just about understanding technology—it's about unlocking potential. With the right knowledge, you can leverage AI to improve both your personal life and professional endeavors. So, let's embark on this adventure together, demystifying AI and discovering how it can transform our world for the better.

Chapter 1: Understanding AI Fundamentals

AI 101: The Basics and Definitions

Artificial Intelligence (AI) is often seen as an abstract concept, but at its core, it represents the pursuit of creating machines that can perform tasks typically requiring human intelligence. These tasks encompass a range of activities, including learning from experiences, understanding natural language, recognizing patterns, and making decisions based on data. Essentially, AI is about developing algorithms that enable computers to process information in ways that mimic human cognitive functions.

Historically, the roots of AI can be traced back to ancient myths and philosophical inquiries into the nature of intelligence. However, the formal birth of AI as a distinct field began in 1956 at the Dartmouth Conference. This landmark event brought together visionaries like John McCarthy and Marvin Minsky, who laid the groundwork for what would evolve into a dynamic and rapidly advancing discipline. They aimed to explore whether machines could simulate aspects of human intelligence, igniting a journey that has since taken many twists and turns.

In the early stages, AI research focused on creating systems capable of solving mathematical problems and playing games like chess. These initial successes were promising, leading to high expectations. However, by the 1970s and 1980s, the field faced a downturn known as the "AI winter," characterized by dwindling funding and interest due to unmet promises. Yet, the emergence of the internet and exponential increases in computing power in the late 1990s rejuvenated the field, setting the stage for breakthroughs in machine learning and data analysis.

Today, we find ourselves in an era where AI is woven into the fabric of our daily lives. With advancements in deep learning and big data analytics, AI technologies have permeated various sectors, from healthcare to entertainment. This rapid evolution reflects not just technological progress but also an expanding understanding of how AI can be applied to solve complex problems. The journey of AI is ongoing, with exciting potential yet to be realized.

Key Points:

- **Definition of AI:** Simulation of human intelligence processes by machines.
- **Historical milestones:** From early algorithms to modern deep learning advancements.

Types of AI: What's the Difference?

AI is not a one-size-fits-all concept; it encompasses various types that serve different purposes. Broadly, AI can be categorized into two main types: Narrow AI and General AI. Understanding these distinctions is crucial for anyone looking to engage with AI technologies meaningfully.

Narrow AI, also referred to as Weak AI, involves systems designed for specific tasks. These systems excel at performing their designated functions but lack the capacity to think or reason outside their programmed limits. For instance, voice assistants like Siri and Google Assistant can process and respond to queries effectively, but they do not possess general intelligence or the ability to engage in conversation outside their programming. Similarly, recommendation systems used by platforms like Netflix and Amazon are tailored to analyze user behavior and suggest content accordingly.

On the other hand, General AI, often referred to as Strong AI, remains largely theoretical. It represents machines that possess the ability to understand, learn, and apply intelligence across a wide range of tasks, mirroring human capabilities. While we are not yet at the point of achieving General AI, the concept raises critical questions about the future of technology and its potential implications for society. Discussions surrounding General AI often evoke excitement and concern, as they touch upon the possibilities of machines with human-like reasoning and emotional understanding.

Ongoing research in AI continues to challenge our understanding of intelligence itself. As we advance, it is essential to consider the ethical implications and the potential impact of these technologies on our lives. Whether we are leveraging Narrow AI for specific tasks or dreaming of a future with General AI, understanding these distinctions helps to frame our expectations and interactions with this transformative technology.

Key Points:

- **Narrow AI:** Specialized systems focused on specific tasks.
- **General AI:** Theoretical concept representing human-like intelligence.

Busting Common Myths

As you embark on your journey to understand AI, it's essential to dispel common misconceptions that often cloud our understanding of the technology. One of the most pervasive myths is that AI can replicate human intelligence entirely. While AI systems can process vast amounts of data and make decisions quickly, they fundamentally lack consciousness, emotions, and the nuanced understanding that characterizes human thought.

Understanding the limits of AI is crucial. AI excels in structured environments with clear rules, such as playing chess or analyzing data patterns. However, it struggles in ambiguous situations that require emotional intelligence or ethical reasoning. For example, while an AI system can analyze medical data to suggest a diagnosis, it cannot understand the emotional weight of delivering that diagnosis to a patient. This gap underscores the importance of human oversight in AI applications, particularly in fields like healthcare and law.

Another myth that needs addressing is the belief that AI will inevitably lead to widespread job losses. While it's true that AI can automate certain tasks, it is equally important to recognize that it also creates new roles and industries requiring human skills, especially in creativity, emotional intelligence, and critical thinking. Rather than replacing humans, AI is designed to augment human capabilities, allowing us to make better decisions and increase productivity in various sectors.

As we explore the landscape of AI, it's essential to approach it with a balanced perspective. Embracing AI as a tool that can enhance our lives, rather than viewing it as a threat, enables us to harness its potential positively. By busting these myths, we can better appreciate the real capabilities and limitations of AI, setting the stage for meaningful engagement with this transformative technology.

Key Points:

- **AI is not human:** Lacks consciousness and emotional understanding.
- **Job displacement vs. creation:** AI will transform the job landscape, not just eliminate jobs.

AI in Your Daily Life

AI isn't a distant technology; it's intricately woven into the fabric of our everyday lives, often in ways we don't even notice. From the moment you wake up to your smart alarm to the personalized recommendations you receive on streaming platforms, AI enhances our experiences in countless ways. Understanding how AI integrates into our lives can help demystify the technology and highlight its benefits.

One of the most significant ways AI impacts our daily routines is through smart home devices. Devices like smart thermostats learn your habits to optimize energy use, providing comfort while saving on utility bills. Imagine returning home to a house that's already warmed or cooled to your preferred temperature. This not only enhances convenience but also promotes energy efficiency, reflecting a growing trend toward sustainability in technology.

Health monitoring is another critical area where AI is making a difference. Wearable devices like fitness trackers and smartwatches provide real-time insights into your physical activity, heart rate, and sleep patterns. These tools empower individuals to take control of their health by encouraging healthier habits and alerting them to potential health changes. For example, an AI-enabled app can analyze your sleep data and provide personalized tips for improving sleep quality, ultimately leading to a healthier lifestyle.

Beyond individual use, AI is transforming industries through its applications in customer service and content creation. Chatbots provide instant responses to inquiries, making customer service more efficient and freeing up human agents for more complex tasks. In creative fields, AI algorithms assist in generating articles, music, and even art, expanding creative possibilities and pushing the boundaries of traditional creativity.

Key Points:

- **Ubiquity of AI:** Present in smart homes, health devices, and customer service.
- **Seamless integration:** Enhancing everyday experiences without being intrusive.

Summary

As we conclude this chapter, it's vital to appreciate that understanding AI fundamentals is your gateway to exploring its profound impact on our lives. From its rich history and various types to the myths that often cloud our perceptions, you are now equipped with foundational knowledge of AI. This understanding not only demystifies the technology but also empowers you to engage with it thoughtfully.

The journey of AI is ongoing, filled with exciting possibilities and ethical considerations. As we move forward, the subsequent chapters will delve deeper into how AI works, explore its practical applications, and equip you with the tools to navigate this transformative landscape effectively. Embrace this journey with curiosity and get ready to discover how AI can enhance your life and work!

Chapter 2: How AI Works

Core Components Made Simple

To truly grasp how AI operates, it's essential to break it down into its core components: algorithms and data. These elements form the foundation of every AI system, working together to create intelligent behavior.

Algorithms: The Secret Sauce

At the heart of AI are algorithms—sets of rules or instructions that guide the machine's behavior. Think of algorithms as the recipe that dictates how AI processes information. They can range from simple if-then statements to complex mathematical functions. The sophistication of an algorithm often determines how effectively an AI can learn from data and make decisions.

One of the most popular types of algorithms in AI is machine learning, which allows systems to learn from data patterns without being explicitly programmed. For example, a recommendation system on a streaming platform analyzes your viewing history and suggests new shows based on your preferences. This ability to adapt and improve over time makes machine learning a cornerstone of modern AI.

In addition, AI algorithms can be categorized into supervised, unsupervised, and reinforcement learning. Each type serves different purposes and has unique strengths, which we will explore further in this chapter. By understanding the role of algorithms, you can appreciate how they enable machines to perform tasks that once seemed exclusive to human intelligence.

Key Points:

- **Algorithms are essential:** They dictate how AI systems process information.
- **Machine learning:** A prominent type of algorithm that enables systems to learn from data.

Data: The Fuel for AI Engines

Data is often referred to as the "fuel" for AI engines. Without high-quality data, even the most advanced algorithms can fall flat. Data comes in various forms—text, images, audio, and more—and each type contributes to an AI system's ability to learn and function effectively.

For AI to make accurate predictions or classifications, it needs to be trained on a substantial amount of relevant data. This training process involves feeding the algorithm large datasets so it can identify patterns and make informed decisions. For instance, facial recognition systems are trained on thousands of images to learn how to distinguish between different faces accurately.

Moreover, the quality of data matters just as much as the quantity. Clean, diverse, and well-labeled datasets lead to better-performing AI systems. In contrast, poor-quality data can result in biased outcomes or errors. This highlights the importance of ethical data collection and management practices in the development of AI technologies.

Key Points:

- **Data as fuel:** Quality data is essential for AI performance.
- **Training process:** AI systems learn patterns from large datasets.

Neural Networks Unplugged

One of the most fascinating aspects of AI is the concept of neural networks. These computational models are inspired by the human brain and are pivotal in enabling machines to perform complex tasks like image and speech recognition.

What Are They and How Do They Work?

Neural networks consist of layers of interconnected nodes or "neurons." Each neuron processes input data, applies a mathematical operation, and passes the output to the next layer. The first layer receives the raw data, while the final layer produces the output, such as a classification or prediction.

Each connection between neurons has a weight that influences how signals are transmitted. During training, the network adjusts these weights based on the error of its predictions, allowing it to learn from its mistakes. This process is known as backpropagation, where the network continuously refines its weights to minimize prediction errors.

Neural networks excel in recognizing patterns within data, making them ideal for tasks like image classification and natural language processing. They are a fundamental component of deep learning, a subset of machine learning that utilizes complex architectures to process large amounts of data.

Key Points:

- **Neural networks mimic the brain:** They consist of layers of interconnected nodes.
- **Learning through backpropagation:** Adjusting weights based on prediction errors improves accuracy.

Training Models: A Learning Journey

Training a neural network is akin to guiding a student through a learning journey. Initially, the network starts with random weights, making wild guesses when trying to predict outcomes. As it encounters more data, it learns from its mistakes, gradually improving its performance.

The training process involves several epochs, where the entire dataset is passed through the network multiple times. With each epoch, the network refines its understanding and enhances its predictive abilities. This iterative process highlights the importance of patience and continuous learning in AI development.

Moreover, the choice of data and the training methodology can significantly impact a model's performance. Techniques such as data augmentation and dropout help enhance the robustness of the model, preventing overfitting—where the model learns to perform well on training data but fails to generalize to new, unseen data.

Key Points:

- **Training involves multiple epochs:** The model improves with each pass through the dataset.
- **Continuous learning:** Iterative processes allow for refinement and adaptation.

Different Learning Styles in AI

AI employs various learning styles to achieve its goals, each with distinct methodologies and applications. Understanding these styles helps demystify how machines learn and adapt to new information.

Supervised Learning

Supervised learning is akin to having a tutor guide a student through specific examples. In this approach, the AI is trained on a labeled dataset, meaning that the input data comes with corresponding output labels. For instance, if you're training a model to recognize cats in images, you would provide it with a dataset of images labeled as "cat" or "not cat."

The algorithm learns by comparing its predictions to the true labels, adjusting its internal parameters to minimize errors. This process continues until the model achieves a satisfactory level of accuracy. Supervised learning is widely used in applications such as email filtering, fraud detection, and image recognition.

Prompt Examples:

- "Classify these images into categories: cat, dog, and other."
- "Given this email, determine if it's spam or not."
- "Predict the price of this house based on its features: location, size, and amenities."

Bad Prompt Examples:

- "Tell me about this image." (Lacks specificity)
- "What is this email about?" (Too vague for classification)
- "Estimate a price." (Without context or features)

Key Points:

- **Supervised learning:** Involves training on labeled datasets with known outputs.
- **Common applications:** Email filtering, image recognition.

Unsupervised Learning

Unsupervised learning, on the other hand, is like exploring a new environment without a map. In this approach, the AI is provided with unlabeled data and tasked with identifying patterns or groupings within that data. This could involve clustering similar data points or discovering hidden structures in a dataset.

For example, customer segmentation in marketing can be achieved through unsupervised learning by analyzing purchasing behaviors and grouping similar customers together. This helps businesses tailor their strategies and offerings to meet the needs of specific customer segments.

Prompt Examples:

- "Group these customer profiles based on purchasing behavior."
- "Identify patterns in this set of unlabeled images."
- "Cluster these articles by topic without prior labels."

Bad Prompt Examples:

- "What's the most interesting pattern?" (Subjective and vague)
- "Find me something useful." (Lacks clear direction)
- "Analyze this data." (Too general without specific guidance)

Key Points:

- **Unsupervised learning:** Involves analyzing unlabeled data to find patterns.
- **Applications:** Customer segmentation, anomaly detection.

Reinforcement Learning: A Fun Breakdown

Reinforcement learning takes a different approach by employing a trial-and-error methodology, much like training a pet. In this paradigm, the AI agent learns to make decisions by interacting with its environment and receiving feedback in the form of rewards or penalties. The agent explores different actions to discover which ones yield the best outcomes.

For instance, in a video game scenario, an AI character learns to navigate through challenges by trying various strategies, receiving positive feedback for successful moves and negative feedback for mistakes. Over time, the agent becomes adept at maximizing its rewards, optimizing its strategy for better performance.

Reinforcement learning has found applications in various fields, including robotics, autonomous vehicles, and game playing. Its ability to adapt to dynamic environments and improve through experience makes it a powerful tool in the AI toolkit.

Prompt Examples:

- "Train this AI to navigate a maze, rewarding it for reaching the exit."
- "Adjust the strategy of a character in a game based on its success rate."
- "Implement a feedback system to enhance the learning of an agent in a simulation."

Bad Prompt Examples:

- "Just try to win." (Lacks specific goals)
- "Do whatever you think is best." (Too vague for effective learning)
- "Get better at this game." (No clear feedback mechanisms)

Key Points:

- **Reinforcement learning:** Learning through trial and error in dynamic environments.

- **Applications:** Robotics, autonomous vehicles, and gaming.

Summary

As we wrap up this chapter, we've uncovered the intricate workings of AI, from its core components—algorithms and data—to the fascinating structures of neural networks. By demystifying concepts like supervised, unsupervised, and reinforcement learning, we've gained valuable insights into how machines learn and adapt.

This foundational knowledge sets the stage for exploring AI's practical applications in the next chapter. Understanding how AI operates empowers you to engage with this transformative technology more confidently, paving the way for deeper exploration in your AI journey. Embrace the excitement of learning and the potential of AI as we continue this adventure together!

Chapter 3: Practical Applications for Everyday Use

AI is not just a futuristic concept; it's a practical tool that enhances our daily lives in numerous ways. From smart assistants that simplify our routines to AI-driven applications in health and business, understanding how to leverage these technologies can significantly improve your everyday experiences. This chapter explores how AI integrates into personal life, entertainment, health, and business, providing you with actionable insights and prompts to make the most of these tools.

Using AI in Personal Life, Entertainment, and Leisure

AI has seamlessly woven itself into our personal lives, making tasks easier, more efficient, and often more enjoyable. Smart assistants like Amazon's Alexa, Google Assistant, and Apple's Siri have transformed how we interact with technology. These virtual helpers perform various tasks, from setting reminders to controlling smart home devices, allowing you to spend more time on what truly matters. The convenience they offer is not just about saving time; it's about creating a more manageable and enjoyable daily routine.

Imagine waking up in the morning and asking your smart assistant for the day's weather, scheduling your coffee to brew at a specific time, and adjusting your home's temperature — all with simple voice commands. This level of integration can streamline your mornings and set a positive tone for the rest of your day. Furthermore, as you become accustomed to using these tools, they learn your preferences, making their suggestions increasingly personalized and relevant.

1. Smart Assistants and Home Automation

Smart assistants serve as your daily companions, ready to help you with tasks that save time and energy. These tools can manage everything from your calendar to your home environment. Picture walking into your home and simply saying, "Turn on the lights" or "Play my favorite playlist." This level of convenience transforms mundane activities into effortless actions, allowing you to focus on what really matters.

Most Common Uses:

- **Task management:** Setting reminders and managing schedules.Prompts: "Set a reminder for my meeting at 2 PM."Prompts: "What's on my agenda for today?"
- **Home control:** Managing smart devices for comfort and efficiency.Prompts: "Adjust the thermostat to 70 degrees."Prompts: "Turn off the living room lights."
- **Information retrieval:** Quick access to news, weather, and trivia.Prompts: "What's the weather forecast for tomorrow?"Prompts: "Tell me the latest news headlines."
- **Entertainment management:** Controlling media playback and selections.Prompts: "Play my favorite playlist on Spotify."Prompts: "Pause the movie."
- **Cooking assistance:** Getting recipe help and cooking tips.Prompts: "Find me a recipe for chicken curry."Prompts: "How long do I bake a potato?"

Bad Prompts:

- "Do everything for me." (Vague and lacks specificity)
- "Make my dinner." (Unclear about what type of dinner or dietary restrictions)
- "Just tell me stuff." (Too broad and non-informative)

Unique AI Prompts:

- "Create a grocery list based on my usual purchases."
- "Tell me a joke to lighten my mood."
- "What's the weather like today, and do I need an umbrella?"

2. AI in Daily Productivity Apps and Creative Tools

AI enhances productivity apps, making them smarter and more intuitive. Tools like Microsoft Office and Google Workspace leverage AI to help with everything from grammar checks to content suggestions. This capability allows you to focus more on your ideas rather than the nitty-gritty details of formatting or proofreading. The result is a more fluid and efficient workflow that empowers creativity.

Imagine writing an email or report, and as you type, AI algorithms suggest enhancements to your text. These features not only improve your writing but also help you learn as you go. You can see examples of effective phrasing and grammar in real time, gradually building your skills without even trying. Furthermore, many productivity apps now incorporate features like smart scheduling and automated reminders, reducing the cognitive load of remembering every task.

Most Common Uses:

- **Document creation:** AI suggests grammar corrections and style improvements.Prompts: "Check my grammar and suggest improvements."Prompts: "What's a better way to phrase this sentence?"
- **Creative design:** AI tools streamline design processes.Prompts: "Generate a color palette for my presentation."Prompts: "Design a social media post based on my content."
- **Meeting scheduling:** AI can help coordinate meeting times based on participants' availability.Prompts: "Find a time for a meeting with John and Sarah."Prompts: "Schedule a weekly check-in on Thursdays."
- **Email management:** AI can sort and prioritize emails based on importance.Prompts: "Organize my inbox by priority."Prompts: "Flag

important emails from this week."
- **Task reminders:** Setting reminders for important deadlines or to-dos.Prompts: "Remind me to send the report by Friday."Prompts: "Notify me about my presentation due next week."

Bad Prompts:

- "Fix my document." (Too vague; does not specify what needs fixing)
- "Make my life easier." (Ambiguous and lacks focus)
- "Help me with everything." (Unrealistic expectations)

Unique AI Prompts:

- "Brainstorm five unique blog post ideas on digital marketing."
- "Create an infographic based on these statistics."
- "Help me outline my presentation for next week."

AI for Health and Wellness

AI is revolutionizing health and wellness, providing tools that empower individuals to take control of their health. From fitness trackers to mental health apps, these innovations make personalized health insights accessible and actionable. The goal is to promote well-being in a way that feels supportive and engaging, rather than overwhelming.

Fitness trackers, for example, are no longer just pedometers; they monitor heart rates, sleep patterns, and even stress levels. By providing real-time feedback, these devices motivate users to reach their fitness goals, whether that's running a marathon or simply walking more each day. The integration of AI allows for personalized recommendations based on individual activity levels and health data.

1. Fitness Trackers and Personalized Health Insights

AI-driven fitness trackers collect data about your physical activities, sleep patterns, and more, offering insights tailored to your unique health needs. These devices can help set and achieve personal fitness goals, making exercise more motivating and effective. Imagine receiving notifications that encourage you to move when you've been inactive for too long, or personalized workout suggestions based on your fitness history.

The analysis goes beyond just numbers. Many fitness trackers can generate trends and patterns over time, showing you how your habits impact your health. This way, you're not just guessing what works for you; you're guided by data. Over time, you can see improvements and make adjustments to your routines, all thanks to the insights provided by your AI-driven tools.

Most Common Uses:

- **Activity tracking:** Monitoring steps, workouts, and heart rate.Prompts: "Track my daily steps."Prompts: "How many calories did I burn during my workout?"
- **Health insights:** Providing personalized feedback on health trends.Prompts: "What's my average sleep quality this week?"Prompts: "Analyze my activity patterns over the past month."
- **Goal setting:** Helping you set and track fitness goals.Prompts: "Set a goal to run 5 miles this week."Prompts: "How close am I to my weight loss goal?"
- **Nutritional tracking:** Logging food intake and providing dietary suggestions.Prompts: "Log my breakfast today."Prompts: "What's my daily calorie intake?"
- **Sleep monitoring:** Analyzing sleep quality and patterns.Prompts: "How many hours did I sleep last night?"Prompts: "What can I do to improve my sleep?"

Bad Prompts:

- "Tell me how to lose weight fast." (Potentially unhealthy and unrealistic)
- "Make me fit." (Unclear expectations)
- "Analyze everything." (Overwhelming and too broad)

Unique AI Prompts:

- "Suggest a weekly workout plan based on my fitness level."
- "Alert me when I've been inactive for too long."
- "What should my hydration goals be based on my activity level?"

2. Mental Health Apps

AI also plays a crucial role in mental health support. Apps that utilize AI can offer personalized coping strategies, mindfulness exercises, and even chat-based support, making mental health resources more accessible. The stigma surrounding mental health is gradually diminishing, and AI-driven applications are at the forefront of making support more available and user-friendly.

These apps can analyze user interactions to provide tailored suggestions, guiding users toward resources that resonate with their specific needs. For instance, if a user frequently logs feelings of anxiety, the app might suggest specific exercises or meditations designed to help mitigate those feelings. This level of personalization not only helps individuals feel seen but also empowers them to take actionable steps toward better mental health.

Most Common Uses:

- **Mindfulness training:** Providing guided meditation sessions.Prompts: "Guide me through a 10-minute meditation."Prompts: "What's a good breathing exercise for stress relief?"
- **Emotional tracking:** Helping users monitor and understand their emotions.Prompts: "How do I feel today?"Prompts: "What triggered my anxiety this week?"
- **Coping strategies:** Offering personalized suggestions based on mood logs.Prompts: "What should I do when I feel anxious?"Prompts: "Give me tips for managing stress."
- **Community support:** Connecting users with online support groups.Prompts: "Find a support group for anxiety."Prompts: "What forums are available for mental health discussions?"

- **Cognitive Behavioral Therapy (CBT) tools:** Facilitating self-help exercises based on CBT principles.Prompts: "Help me reframe negative thoughts."Prompts: "What are some strategies to challenge my anxiety?"

Bad Prompts:

- "Fix my mental health." (Overly simplistic and unrealistic)
- "Tell me how to be happy." (Lacks specific context)
- "Make my problems go away." (Unrealistic expectations)

Unique AI Prompts:

- "Suggest a daily gratitude practice for me."
- "What are some techniques to manage intrusive thoughts?"
- "Provide an overview of my mood trends over the last month."

AI Revolutionizing Businesses and Creative Industries

AI is not only a personal companion but also a powerful tool for businesses. Its ability to analyze data, automate tasks, and improve efficiency is transforming industries across the board. From streamlining operations to generating insights, AI is a game changer that can drive success in today's competitive landscape.

Companies that harness the power of AI can improve productivity and gain a significant edge over competitors. By automating repetitive tasks, businesses can focus on innovation and strategic planning rather than being bogged down by administrative work. Moreover, AI can sift through massive datasets to find trends and insights that would be impossible for a human to uncover in a reasonable time frame.

1. Automation and Efficiency: Your New Best Friend

One of the most significant impacts of AI on businesses is automation. By automating routine tasks, businesses can save time and reduce errors. For instance, AI can handle data entry, customer support inquiries, and even inventory management, allowing employees to focus on more valuable tasks. This shift not only increases productivity but also enhances job satisfaction, as employees can engage in more meaningful work.

Imagine a scenario where your customer service inquiries are handled by an AI chatbot. This technology can address common questions 24/7, freeing up human agents to deal with more complex issues. As a result, response times improve, and customer satisfaction rises. Moreover, AI can continuously learn from interactions, becoming more effective at resolving issues over time.

Most Common Uses:

- **Customer service:** AI chatbots handling inquiries and providing support.Prompts: "What are the most common customer inquiries?"Prompts: "Resolve this customer issue."
- **Data entry automation:** Streamlining repetitive tasks.Prompts: "Input this data into our CRM system."Prompts: "Update our inventory records."
- **Email sorting:** Managing inboxes and prioritizing important messages.Prompts: "Organize my emails by urgency."Prompts: "Filter out spam emails."
- **Lead generation:** Identifying and qualifying potential customers.Prompts: "Find leads based on recent engagement."Prompts: "What's the status of our current leads?"
- **Project management:** Automating task assignments and tracking progress.Prompts: "Assign tasks to team members based on availability." Prompts: "Generate a project status report."

Bad Prompts:

- "Make my business successful." (Too broad and unrealistic)
- "Handle everything for me." (Lacks specific context)
- "Fix my customer service." (Too vague)

Unique AI Prompts:

- "Identify the top customer concerns from this month's data."
- "Automate the onboarding process for new clients."
- "Create a workflow to manage project deadlines."

2. Data Analytics: Making Sense of It All

In today's data-driven world, the ability to analyze vast amounts of information quickly is invaluable. AI enables businesses to extract meaningful insights from complex datasets, allowing for informed decision-making. This capability can lead to improved strategies, better understanding of customer needs, and identification of new market opportunities.

For instance, predictive analytics can forecast future trends based on historical data, guiding businesses in their strategic planning. By understanding customer behavior and market dynamics, companies can tailor their offerings and marketing strategies, ultimately enhancing customer satisfaction and loyalty. The ability to turn data into actionable insights is a powerful advantage in a competitive market.

Most Common Uses:

- **Market analysis:** Understanding trends and customer preferences.Prompts: "What are the current market trends in our industry?"Prompts: "Analyze customer feedback from the last quarter."
- **Performance tracking:** Monitoring KPIs and business health.Prompts: "Show me this month's sales performance."Prompts: "What's our customer retention rate?"
- **Predictive analytics:** Forecasting future trends based on historical data.Prompts: "What will our sales look like next quarter?"Prompts: "Predict customer behavior for the upcoming holiday season."
- **Segmentation analysis:** Understanding different customer demographics.Prompts: "Group customers by purchase behavior."Prompts: "Identify high-value customers based on spending."
- **Competitor analysis:** Keeping tabs on competitors' activities and performance.Prompts: "What strategies are our competitors using?"Prompts: "Analyze competitor pricing strategies."

Bad Prompts:

- "Tell me everything." (Overwhelming and unrealistic)
- "What do I do with this data?" (Lacks direction)
- "Find me the best solution." (Too vague)

Unique AI Prompts:

- "Predict next quarter's sales based on historical data."
- "Identify the top three areas for improvement in customer satisfaction."
- "Create a visual dashboard of our key performance metrics."

In summary, AI is a transformative force enhancing various aspects of our lives, from personal tasks and health management to business efficiency and creativity. By understanding these practical applications and utilizing the prompts provided, you can unlock the full potential of AI in your daily routine, making life easier, more productive, and more enjoyable. Embrace the technology around you, and watch as it enriches your life in ways you never thought possible.

Chapter 4: Overcoming Common Struggles

As you embark on your journey to understand and utilize artificial intelligence, you may encounter various challenges that can feel overwhelming. From complex terminology to translating theoretical concepts into practical applications, these hurdles can hinder your progress. This chapter aims to address these common struggles, providing you with clear explanations, practical examples, and best practices to enhance your experience with AI.

Navigating Terminology and Concepts

The world of AI is filled with jargon and technical terms that can be intimidating for beginners. Understanding these terms is crucial, as they form the foundation of your knowledge. By simplifying terminology, we can make the concepts more approachable and relatable.

AI encompasses a variety of terms, such as "machine learning," "neural networks," and "natural language processing." While these may sound complicated, breaking them down into simpler definitions can help demystify the subject. For example, machine learning refers to the ability of a computer to learn from data and improve its performance over time without being explicitly programmed. It's a core component of AI that drives many applications you encounter daily.

1. Simplifying Key Terms

To facilitate your understanding, let's clarify some of the most common terms you'll encounter in AI discussions:

- **Artificial Intelligence (AI):** The simulation of human intelligence in machines to perform tasks that typically require human-like cognitive functions.
- **Machine Learning (ML):** A subset of AI that enables systems to learn from data and improve their performance without explicit programming.
- **Deep Learning:** A form of machine learning that uses neural networks with multiple layers to analyze complex data patterns.
- **Natural Language Processing (NLP):** The field of AI that focuses on enabling computers to understand and interact using human language.
- **Neural Networks:** Computational models inspired by the human brain, designed to recognize patterns in data through interconnected nodes.
- **Supervised Learning:** A type of machine learning where a model is trained on labeled data, learning to predict outcomes based on input-output pairs.
- **Unsupervised Learning:** A machine learning approach where a model analyzes unlabeled data to identify patterns and group similar data points.
- **Reinforcement Learning:** A learning paradigm where an agent learns to make decisions by receiving rewards or penalties based on its actions in an environment.
- **Data Mining:** The process of discovering patterns and knowledge from large sets of data using statistical and computational techniques.
- **Computer Vision:** A field of AI that enables computers to interpret and understand visual information from the world, such as images and videos.
- **Robotics:** The branch of technology that deals with the design, construction, and operation of robots, often incorporating AI for autonomous decision-making.
- **Chatbot:** An AI program designed to simulate conversation with human users, often used in customer service applications.
- **Recommendation Systems:** Algorithms that analyze user behavior and preferences to suggest products, services, or content, commonly used by platforms like Netflix and Amazon.
- **Predictive Analytics:** The use of statistical algorithms and machine learning techniques to identify the likelihood of future outcomes based on historical data.

- **Feature Extraction:** The process of transforming raw data into a set of characteristics (features) that can be used for machine learning models.
- **Training Data:** The dataset used to train machine learning models, helping them learn to make predictions or decisions.
- **Overfitting:** A modeling error that occurs when a machine learning model learns the training data too well, failing to generalize to new data.
- **Underfitting:** A scenario where a machine learning model is too simple to capture the underlying patterns in the data, resulting in poor performance.
- **Generative Models:** AI models that can generate new data samples that resemble the training data, such as creating realistic images or text.
- **Transfer Learning:** A technique where a pre-trained model is adapted to a new but related task, allowing for faster training and improved performance.
- **Bias in AI:** Systematic errors that result from prejudiced assumptions in the machine learning process, affecting fairness and accuracy.
- **Explainable AI (XAI):** AI systems designed to provide clear and understandable explanations for their decisions and actions.
- **Sentiment Analysis:** The use of NLP to determine the emotional tone behind a series of words, often used in social media monitoring and customer feedback.
- **Autonomous Systems:** Machines or software that can perform tasks without human intervention, often leveraging AI for decision-making.
- **AI Ethics:** The field of study that addresses the moral implications and responsibilities associated with the development and use of artificial intelligence technologies.
- **Algorithm:** A set of rules or calculations used to solve problems or perform tasks, forming the basis of AI models.
- **Data Augmentation:** Techniques used to increase the diversity of training data without actually collecting new data, often used in image processing.
- **Hyperparameters:** Settings or configurations that are used to control the learning process of machine learning algorithms, which can significantly affect performance.
- **Regularization:** A technique used to prevent overfitting in machine

learning models by adding a penalty for complexity.
- **Cross-Validation:** A statistical method used to estimate the skill of machine learning models by dividing the data into subsets for training and testing.
- **Natural Language Generation (NLG):** A subfield of NLP focused on generating human-like text from structured data.
- **Speech Recognition:** The ability of AI systems to recognize and process human speech, converting it into text or commands.
- **Clustering:** An unsupervised learning technique that groups similar data points together based on certain features, often used in market segmentation.
- **Dimensionality Reduction:** Techniques used to reduce the number of input variables in a dataset, making models simpler and faster while retaining essential information.
- **Anomaly Detection:** The identification of rare items, events, or observations that raise suspicions by differing significantly from the majority of the data.
- **Tokenization:** The process of breaking text into smaller pieces, or tokens, which can be individual words or phrases, often used in NLP.
- **Contextual Understanding:** The ability of AI systems to understand the context in which words or phrases are used, improving comprehension and response accuracy.
- **Generative Adversarial Networks (GANs):** A class of machine learning frameworks where two neural networks compete against each other to generate new data samples.
- **Synthetic Data:** Artificially generated data that mimics real-world data, used for training AI models without privacy concerns.
- **AI Model:** A mathematical representation of a real-world process or system, created through training on data.
- **Inference:** The process of using a trained model to make predictions or decisions based on new, unseen data.
- **Transfer Function:** A mathematical function that describes the input-output relationship of a system, often used in neural networks.

- **Precision and Recall:** Metrics used to evaluate the performance of a model, where precision measures the accuracy of positive predictions, and recall measures the ability to identify all relevant instances.
- **Semantic Analysis:** The process of understanding the meaning and interpretation of words, phrases, and sentences in context.
- **Ensemble Learning:** Techniques that combine multiple models to improve overall performance, often resulting in more robust predictions.
- **AI Governance:** The framework of policies and guidelines that ensure responsible and ethical use of AI technologies.
- **Human-in-the-Loop (HITL):** A model design approach where human feedback is integrated into the machine learning process to improve accuracy and performance.
- **Feature Engineering:** The process of selecting, modifying, or creating new features from raw data to improve model performance.
- **Model Evaluation:** The assessment of a machine learning model's performance using various metrics to determine its effectiveness.
- **AI-Powered Automation:** The use of AI technologies to automate processes and tasks, improving efficiency and productivity across industries.

These terms represent fundamental concepts in AI. By familiarizing yourself with them, you can engage more confidently in discussions and further your understanding of the technology.

Key Information:

- Familiarity with basic AI terminology is essential for understanding the field.
- Machine learning is a key component of many AI applications.
- Deep learning and natural language processing are specialized areas of AI.

2. Practical Examples to Illustrate Ideas

To make these concepts more tangible, let's look at practical examples of AI in action. Consider how machine learning algorithms power recommendation systems on platforms like Netflix and Amazon. These systems analyze your viewing or purchasing history and suggest content or products based on your preferences. This is a direct application of machine learning, where the algorithm learns from your behavior to improve user experience.

Another example is natural language processing, which is used in virtual assistants like Siri or Google Assistant. These applications analyze spoken language to understand and respond to user queries, illustrating how AI can bridge the gap between humans and machines.

Key Information:

- AI applications are present in everyday tools like recommendation systems and virtual assistants.
- Practical examples help bridge the gap between theory and reality.
- Understanding AI concepts through real-world applications enhances comprehension.

Translating Theory into Practice

While grasping AI terminology is essential, being able to apply this knowledge in practical scenarios is equally important. Theory alone can feel abstract and detached from everyday life. This section focuses on hands-on activities that can reinforce your understanding of AI concepts and provide a solid foundation for using AI tools.

Engaging with AI through practical activities can help solidify your knowledge and make the learning process more enjoyable. For example, experimenting with free online AI tools can give you firsthand experience in how these systems work. You can explore machine learning platforms like Google's Teachable Machine, which allows you to train a simple model using your own data—like images or sounds.

1. Hands-On Activities to Reinforce Learning

Consider trying out the following hands-on activities:

Experiment with AI Tools

- **Teachable Machine:** A user-friendly tool for creating machine learning models using your own data (images, sounds, or poses).
- **Website:** Teachable Machine - https://teachablemachine.withgoogle.com/
- **Runway ML:** A creative suite that provides various AI tools for video editing, image generation, and more.
- **Website:** Runway ML - https://runwayml.com/
- **Google AI Experiments:** A collection of interactive AI experiments that allow you to explore different AI technologies and concepts.
- **Website:** Google AI Experiments - https://experiments.withgoogle.com/collection/ai
- **Lobe:** A free app that helps you train machine learning models using your own images in a visual way.
- **Website:** Lobe - https://www.lobe.ai/
- **PaddlePaddle:** An open-source deep learning platform with tutorials for beginners to experiment with AI models.
- **Website:** PaddlePaddle - https://www.paddlepaddle.org/

Play with Chatbots

- **Chatbot.com:** A platform for building and deploying chatbots with a user-friendly visual interface.
- **Website:** Chatbot.com - https://www.chatbot.com/
- **Dialogflow:** Google's natural language understanding platform for building conversational agents.
- **Website:** Dialogflow - https://dialogflow.cloud.google.com/
- **Botpress:** An open-source framework for creating chatbots, focusing on modularity and flexibility.
- **Website:** Botpress - https://botpress.com/
- **ManyChat:** A platform for building chatbots on Facebook Messenger, Instagram, and SMS with an easy drag-and-drop interface.
- **Website:** ManyChat - https://www.manychat.com/
- **Tidio:** A chatbot platform for websites that combines live chat and bot

responses, enhancing customer engagement.
- **Website:** Tidio - **https://www.tidio.com/**

Data Analysis Projects

- **Kaggle:** A platform offering a variety of datasets for exploration and analysis, along with community-driven projects.
- **Website:** Kaggle - https://www.kaggle.com/datasets
- **Google Dataset Search:** A search engine for datasets across the web, making it easy to find publicly available data.
- **Website:** Google Dataset Search - https://datasetsearch.research.google.com/
- **UCI Machine Learning Repository:** A well-known repository containing a large collection of datasets for machine learning and data analysis.
- **Website:** UCI Repository - **https://archive.ics.uci.edu/ml/index.php**
- **Data.gov:** The U.S. government's open data site, offering access to a wide range of datasets across various domains.
- **Website:** Data.gov - **https://www.data.gov/**
- **Excel Easy:** A website with tutorials on using Excel for data analysis, from basics to advanced functions.
- **Website:** Excel Easy - **https://www.excel-easy.com/**

These resources should provide ample opportunities for hands-on exploration and learning in the areas of AI tools, chatbots, and data analysis!

By actively participating in these activities, you can bridge the gap between theory and practice, gaining confidence in your ability to work with AI concepts and tools.

Key Information:

- Hands-on activities are crucial for reinforcing theoretical concepts.
- Experimenting with AI tools enhances your understanding and builds confidence.
- Engaging with practical projects makes learning enjoyable and memo-

rable.

Best Practices for Using AI Tools

As you gain familiarity with AI terminology and practical applications, it's essential to understand best practices for using AI tools effectively. This knowledge can help you navigate challenges and maximize the benefits of AI in your personal and professional life.

Effective use of AI tools requires a thoughtful approach. Start by clearly defining your goals before diving into an AI tool. Understanding what you want to achieve will guide your interactions with the technology and help you choose the right tools for your needs.

1. Establish Clear Goals

Before using an AI tool, take a moment to think about what you aim to accomplish. Whether it's improving productivity, automating a task, or analyzing data, having clear objectives will help you choose the right tool and use it effectively.

- **Identify your needs:** Determine the specific tasks you want to automate or analyze.
- **Set measurable goals:** Define what success looks like for each task, such as reducing time spent on a process by a certain percentage.

Key Information:

- Clear objectives guide your use of AI tools and improve outcomes.
- Understanding your needs helps you select the right technology.
- Setting measurable goals allows you to track your progress.

2. Stay Informed and Adapt

AI technology is rapidly evolving, and staying updated with the latest trends and tools is essential. Engage with communities and forums, attend webinars, and read articles to enhance your knowledge and skills.

- **Join online communities:** Participate in forums like Reddit's r/MachineLearning or AI-specific groups on social media to share experiences and learn from others.
- **Follow industry news:** Keep up with developments in AI through blogs, podcasts, and newsletters that focus on AI advancements and applications.

By staying informed, you can adapt your strategies and tools to remain effective in an ever-changing landscape.

Key Information:

- Staying informed about AI trends and tools enhances your skillset.
- Engaging with communities fosters learning and collaboration.
- Continuous adaptation ensures effective use of AI technologies.

In summary, overcoming common struggles in learning about AI is entirely achievable with the right resources and approach. By simplifying terminology, translating theory into practice through hands-on activities, and adhering to best practices, you can build a solid foundation for using AI effectively. Embrace the learning journey and remember that every challenge is an opportunity for growth in the exciting world of artificial intelligence.

Chapter 5: Getting Started with AI Tools

Essential AI Tools and Platforms

As you embark on your journey into the world of artificial intelligence, understanding the tools and platforms available is crucial. Fortunately, there are many user-friendly AI applications designed specifically for beginners. These tools can help demystify complex concepts, allowing you to dive in with confidence.

Top 5 User-Friendly AI Applications for Beginners

1. **Teachable Machine**A web-based tool by Google that allows users to create simple machine learning models by uploading images, sounds, or poses. Its intuitive interface makes it easy for anyone to experiment with AI concepts without prior coding experience.*Link: Teachable Machine*
2. **Google Colab**A free, cloud-based Jupyter notebook environment that allows you to write and execute Python code. It is ideal for beginners to experiment with machine learning and data analysis using pre-installed libraries and access to GPU resources.*Link: Google Colab*
3. **Microsoft Azure Machine Learning Studio**A drag-and-drop interface that enables users to build, test, and deploy machine learning models without needing extensive programming knowledge. It provides a variety of pre-built algorithms and datasets.*Link: Azure Machine Learning Studio*
4. **IBM Watson Studio**A comprehensive suite for data science and AI

development that offers a user-friendly interface for building, training, and deploying machine learning models. It includes tools for data visualization and collaboration.*Link: IBM Watson Studio*

5. **Runway ML** A platform designed for creators, allowing users to integrate AI into their artistic projects. It offers a variety of pre-trained models for tasks like image and video generation, making it accessible for artists and designers.*Link: Runway ML*

These resources provide a solid starting point for beginners looking to explore AI without getting overwhelmed by technical complexities.

Key Information:

- Many AI tools offer drag-and-drop functionality, making them accessible to beginners.
- Platforms like Google Colab and Teachable Machine require minimal setup, allowing you to focus on learning.
- The versatility of these tools can cater to a variety of interests, from data analysis to creative projects.

Kickstarting Your First AI Project

Now that you're familiar with some essential tools, it's time to think about your first AI project. Starting small is the key to building confidence and understanding the process involved in AI development. These projects offer a great introduction to AI concepts and practical applications, making it easier for beginners to engage and learn effectively.

Here's a detailed explanation of each of the top 10 simple AI projects for beginners, along with example prompts to get you started:

Image Classification: Use platforms like Teachable Machine to train a model that can classify images into predefined categories. This project helps you understand how machines recognize and categorize visual data.

Example Prompts:

- "Upload images of cats and dogs and train the model to distinguish between them."
- "Create a classification model for different types of fruits."

Chatbot Creation: Build a simple chatbot using tools like Dialogflow or Chatbot.com. This project teaches you about natural language processing and how AI can interact with users through conversation.

Example Prompts:

- "Create a chatbot that answers frequently asked questions about your favorite hobby."
- "Design a chatbot that can help users book appointments."

Sentiment Analysis: Analyze text data (like tweets or product reviews) to determine their sentiment (positive, negative, or neutral). This project utilizes libraries like NLTK or TextBlob to perform text analysis.

Example Prompts:

- "Analyze tweets related to a trending topic to gauge public sentiment."
- "Use product reviews to identify customer feelings about a new gadget."

Personalized Recommendations: Create a basic recommendation system that suggests movies or products based on user preferences. This project introduces you to collaborative filtering and user data analysis.

Example Prompts:

- "Build a movie recommendation system that suggests films based on user ratings."
- "Create a product recommendation engine for an online store using customer purchase history."

Basic Data Visualization: Use datasets from sources like Kaggle to create visualizations that help interpret and communicate data insights. Tools like

Tableau or Python's Matplotlib are great for this.
Example Prompts:

- "Visualize the distribution of ages in a dataset using a histogram."
- "Create a pie chart showing the market share of different smartphone brands."

Voice Assistant: Develop a simple voice assistant using Python with libraries like Speech Recognition and pyttsx3 to convert text to speech. This project introduces voice recognition and response generation.
Example Prompts:

- "Create a voice assistant that can tell you the weather for the day."
- "Build a simple assistant that sets reminders based on voice commands."

Handwritten Digit Recognition: Use the MNIST dataset to train a neural network that recognizes handwritten digits. This project allows you to explore deep learning concepts using TensorFlow or Keras.
Example Prompts:

- "Train a model to identify handwritten numbers from 0 to 9."
- "Test your model by providing it with new handwritten digit samples."

Stock Price Prediction: Create a basic model to predict stock prices using historical data. This project applies regression techniques to financial data analysis.
Example Prompts:

- "Use historical stock data to predict future prices using linear regression."
- "Analyze trends in stock prices for a specific company over the past year."

Image Style Transfer: Experiment with neural networks to transfer artistic styles from one image to another. This project uses deep learning techniques

to merge different artistic styles.
Example Prompts:

- "Apply the style of a famous painting to a personal photo."
- "Create a new artwork by blending two distinct images together."

Text Generation: Use simple algorithms or models to generate text based on input prompts. This project helps you explore natural language generation using tools like GPT-2 or RNNs.
Example Prompts:

- "Generate a short story based on the prompt 'a journey through time.'"
- "Create a poem by providing a theme or first line."

Step-by-Step Adventure Guide

This step-by-step guide provides a clear path for beginners to follow, ensuring that they not only engage with AI tools effectively but also derive meaningful insights and experiences from their projects.

Choose Your Project
Identify which of the simple projects excites you the most.

- **Explore Options:** Start by reviewing the list of simple AI projects provided earlier. Consider factors like your interests (e.g., music, art, gaming) and your familiarity with the subject matter.
- **Assess Your Skills:** Think about your current skill level. If you're a complete beginner, you might want to start with a project that requires minimal coding or technical knowledge, such as a chatbot or data visualization.
- **Make a Decision:** Once you've considered your interests and skill level, choose a project that feels engaging and achievable. For example, if you love movies, a personalized recommendation system could be the perfect

fit.

Research and Resources

Gather any resources you might need, including datasets or templates.

- **Identify Required Tools:** Depending on your project, you might need specific software or platforms. For instance, if you're building a chatbot, you may want to use tools like Dialogflow or Botpress.
- **Collect Data:** If your project involves data analysis or machine learning, look for relevant datasets. Websites like Kaggle, UCI Machine Learning Repository, and Google Dataset Search are excellent places to find data.
- **Learn the Basics:** Before diving in, spend some time learning the basics of the tools you'll use. Look for tutorials or documentation that can provide a solid foundation. For example, if you're using TensorFlow, check out their official tutorials on YouTube or their website.
- **Create a Checklist:** Make a list of all the resources, datasets, and tools you'll need, so you have everything at your fingertips when you start building.

Build and Test

Follow the guides provided by the tool you've chosen and iterate on your project based on your findings.

- **Start Building:** Using the resources you've gathered, begin constructing your project. Follow step-by-step tutorials carefully, ensuring you understand each step. If something isn't clear, don't hesitate to look for additional resources or ask for help online.
- **Test as You Go:** As you build, regularly test your work. This means running your code, checking outputs, or interacting with your model. If you're working on a chatbot, for instance, engage with it frequently to see how it responds to various inputs.
- **Iterate and Improve:** Don't be afraid to make changes and refine your project. If something isn't working as expected, troubleshoot and adjust

your approach. For example, if your image classification model isn't accurate, consider revising your dataset or experimenting with different algorithms.
- **Document Your Process:** Keep notes on what you do and learn throughout the building process. This documentation can be invaluable for troubleshooting and for sharing your project later.

Reflect and Share

Once completed, reflect on what you learned and consider sharing your project with a community for feedback.

- **Take Time to Reflect:** After finishing your project, spend some time reflecting on the experience. Consider questions like: What challenges did I face? What skills did I develop? What would I do differently next time?
- **Seek Feedback:** Sharing your project can be an excellent way to gain new insights. Consider posting your work on platforms like GitHub, Medium, or relevant forums. Engage with communities on Reddit, Discord, or LinkedIn groups dedicated to AI and machine learning.
- **Prepare a Presentation:** If you're sharing your project publicly, think about how to present your work effectively. Create a brief write-up or video that showcases what you built, the process you followed, and the results you achieved.
- **Set Future Goals:** Based on your reflections and the feedback you receive, consider setting goals for your next steps in learning AI. This could involve tackling a more complex project or exploring a new area of AI that piqued your interest during this project.

Essential Resources and Datasets

Finding the right datasets and resources is crucial for any AI project, especially for beginners. Here's an expanded list of essential resources, complete with examples and links, to help you kick start your projects effectively.

Kaggle Datasets

Kaggle is a well-known platform for data science and machine learning. It offers a vast repository of datasets, along with kernels (code notebooks) where users can share their work and insights. For example: View Datasets at https://www.kaggle.com/datasets

- Titanic Dataset: A classic dataset used for classification tasks, predicting survival based on various features.
- House Prices: A dataset for regression tasks to predict house prices based on various factors.
- Fashion MNIST: A dataset for image classification, featuring 70,000 images of clothing items.

UCI Machine Learning Repository

The UCI Machine Learning Repository is a collection of databases, domain theories, and datasets widely used by the machine learning community. For example:

- Iris Dataset: A simple yet famous dataset for classification tasks involving flower species. View Dataset https://archive.ics.uci.edu/ml/datasets/iris
- Wine Quality: A dataset for regression and classification tasks, predicting the quality of wines based on physicochemical tests. View Dataset https://archive.ics.uci.edu/ml/datasets/wine+quality
- Adult Income Dataset: A dataset for predicting whether individuals earn more or less than $50K per year. View Dataset https://archive.ics.uci.edu/ml/datasets/adult

Google Dataset Search

Google Dataset Search allows users to find datasets stored across the web. It's a powerful tool to discover datasets relevant to your specific interests. For example:

- **How to Use:** Simply enter keywords related to your topic of interest to find relevant datasets. https://datasetsearch.research.google.com/

Data.gov

Data.gov is a comprehensive platform that provides access to thousands of datasets from the U.S. government. It covers a wide array of topics, from climate to health. For example:

- COVID-19 Data: Datasets related to the pandemic, including case counts and vaccination data. Explore COVID-19 Datasets https://covid.data.gov/
- Climate Data: Climate datasets from NOAA, providing insights into temperature changes and weather patterns. Explore NOAA https://www.ncdc.noaa.gov/cdo-web/

Awesome Public Datasets

This GitHub repository curates a list of high-quality public datasets across various domains. For example:

- Health: Datasets related to health, including patient data and public health statistics. Explore Health Datasets https://github.com/awesomedata/awesome-public-datasets#health
- Finance: Financial datasets, including stock prices, market trends, and economic indicators. Explore Finance Datasets https://github.com/awesomedata/awesome-public-datasets#finance

Open Data Portal

Many cities and organizations provide open data portals, which offer datasets related to local governance, demographics, and public services. For example:

- NYC Open Data: A collection of datasets from New York City's government, covering everything from transportation to health. Explore NYC Open Data https://opendata.cityofnewyork.us/
- London Datastore: Datasets related to various aspects of life in London, in-

cluding transport, environment, and housing. Explore London Datastore https://data.london.gov.uk/

FiveThirtyEight Datasets

The data journalism site FiveThirtyEight provides various datasets used in their articles, ideal for projects involving statistical analysis. For example:

- US Elections: Datasets related to election outcomes and voter demographics. Explore US Elections Dataset https://data.fivethirtyeight.com/#election
- Sports Data: Datasets for various sports, including NBA and NFL statistics. Explore Sports Data https://data.fivethirtyeight.com/#sports

World Health Organization (WHO) Data

The WHO provides datasets related to global health statistics, disease outbreaks, and healthcare policies. For example:

- Global Health Observatory Data: Data on health-related topics, including disease prevalence and health system statistics. Explore WHO Data https://www.who.int/data/gho

European Union Open Data Portal

The EU Open Data Portal provides access to a wide range of datasets produced by European Union institutions. For example:

- EU Financial Data: Datasets on EU budgets, spending, and economic indicators. Explore EU Financial Data - https://data.europa.eu/en

OpenStreetMap (OSM)

OpenStreetMap offers free geographic data that can be useful for projects involving mapping, geolocation, and spatial analysis. For example:

- Map Data: Access to a rich dataset of maps that can be used for various applications. Explore OpenStreetMap https://www.openstreetmap.org/

Reddit Datasets

A community-driven collection of datasets shared on Reddit, covering a wide array of topics and use cases. For example:

- User-Generated Datasets: Many users share unique datasets they've created or found. Explore Reddit Datasets https://www.reddit.com/r/datasets/

Microsoft Research Open Data

A platform providing datasets curated by Microsoft Research, designed to facilitate research and learning. For example:

- ImageNet: A large dataset for image classification tasks. Explore ImageNet https://www.image-net.org/
- Text Datasets: Various datasets for natural language processing and text analysis. Explore Text Datasets https://msropendata.com/

These resources and datasets will provide you with a solid foundation to embark on your AI projects, offering a variety of options across different domains. Whether you're interested in health, finance, or creative arts, there's likely a dataset out there that fits your needs!

Key Information:

- Start with small, manageable projects to build confidence.
- Utilizing community resources can greatly enhance your learning experience.
- Reflecting on your project helps solidify your understanding.

CHAPTER 5: GETTING STARTED WITH AI TOOLS

Prompt Writing Hacks: Crafting the Perfect Input

A significant part of working with AI involves writing effective prompts. A well-crafted prompt can lead to more accurate results, while a poorly written one may yield irrelevant or confusing outputs.

Tips for Writing Effective Prompts

Crafting effective prompts is essential for harnessing the full potential of AI tools. A well-structured prompt can significantly improve the quality of the AI's responses. Here are the top 10 tips for writing effective prompts:

Be Specific

- **Detail Your Request:** Clearly outline what you want from the AI. Vague prompts can lead to generic answers.
- **Example:** Instead of asking, "Tell me about AI," you could say, "Explain how machine learning is used in healthcare."

Provide Context

- **Set the Scene:** Give the AI background information that can help it understand your request better.
- **Example:** "As a marketing expert, summarize the impact of social media on brand awareness."

Use Clear Language

- **Avoid Jargon:** Use straightforward language to make your prompt accessible.
- **Example:** Instead of using technical terms, say, "What are the benefits of AI in everyday life?"

Ask Open-Ended Questions

- **Encourage Elaborate Responses:** Open-ended questions invite detailed answers rather than yes/no responses.
- **Example:** "What are the potential future applications of AI in education?"

Include Examples

- **Clarify Expectations:** Providing examples can guide the AI in generating relevant responses.
- **Example:** "List three AI applications in agriculture, such as crop monitoring and yield prediction."

Limit the Scope

- **Stay Focused:** Narrow down the subject to prevent overwhelming responses.
- **Example:** "Discuss the role of AI in automated customer service rather than all AI applications."

Iterate on Your Prompts

- **Refine for Clarity:** If the response isn't what you expected, tweak your prompt and try again.
- **Example:** If "Explain neural networks" yields a complex answer, refine it to "What are neural networks in simple terms?"

Specify the Format

- **Desired Structure:** Indicate how you want the information organized.
- **Example:** "Summarize the benefits of AI in bullet points."

Use Role Play

- **Assume Perspectives:** Position the AI in a specific role to generate contextually relevant responses.
- **Example:** "As a personal trainer, suggest a workout plan using AI."

Be Patient

- **Experiment and Adapt:** Don't be discouraged by initial results; effective prompt writing often requires practice.
- **Example:** Try different variations of your request to see what works best.

Examples of Good Prompts

Technology

- "What are the latest trends in AI technology for 2024?"
- "Explain the difference between machine learning and deep learning."
- "How do neural networks mimic human brain functions?"
- "What role does AI play in cybersecurity?"
- "Describe the future of quantum computing and AI."

Health and Wellness

- "How can AI improve mental health treatments?"
- "List five AI applications in fitness tracking."
- "What are the ethical concerns surrounding AI in healthcare?"
- "How can AI assist in diagnosing diseases?"
- "Discuss the role of AI in personalized medicine."

Education

- "As a teacher, how can I integrate AI into my curriculum?"

- "What are the benefits of using AI for personalized learning?"
- "How can AI help in assessing student performance?"
- "Discuss the potential of AI in remote learning environments."
- "What AI tools can enhance classroom engagement?"

Business and Marketing

- "How can small businesses leverage AI for marketing strategies?"
- "Describe the role of AI in customer service automation."
- "What are some successful case studies of AI in e-commerce?"
- "How can AI help with market trend analysis?"
- "Discuss the impact of AI on supply chain management."

Creative Arts

- "What are some AI tools that help artists with their creative process?"
- "Explain how AI is changing the music industry."
- "How can AI be used in filmmaking and video production?"
- "Discuss the intersection of AI and graphic design."
- "What are the implications of AI-generated art?"

Environmental Sustainability

- "How can AI contribute to renewable energy solutions?"
- "Discuss AI applications in wildlife conservation efforts."
- "What role does AI play in climate change modeling?"
- "How can smart farming leverage AI for sustainability?"
- "Explore AI's impact on reducing waste in industries."

Finance

- "What are the risks and rewards of using AI in financial trading?"
- "Explain how AI can enhance personal finance management."

- "How is AI used for fraud detection in banking?"
- "Discuss the future of robo-advisors in wealth management."
- "What are the implications of AI on cryptocurrency markets?"

Travel and Tourism

- "How is AI used to personalize travel recommendations?"
- "What are the benefits of AI in the hospitality industry?"
- "Discuss how AI can optimize flight and hotel pricing."
- "How can AI enhance customer service in travel agencies?"
- "What role does AI play in improving travel safety?"

Sports and Fitness

- "How can AI enhance training programs for athletes?"
- "What role does AI play in sports analytics?"
- "Discuss the use of AI in injury prevention and recovery."
- "How can AI improve fan engagement in sports?"
- "What are the implications of AI in eSports?"

Social Issues

- "Discuss the ethical implications of AI surveillance."
- "How can AI help address bias in hiring practices?"
- "What role does AI play in combating misinformation?"
- "How can AI assist in disaster response and management?"
- "Discuss the challenges of AI regulation and policy."

Entertainment

- "What are the best AI-driven tools for movie recommendations?"
- "How is AI transforming video game development?"
- "Discuss the role of AI in scriptwriting and content creation."

- "What impact does AI have on audience analytics?"
- "How can AI personalize streaming services for users?"

Home and Lifestyle

- "How can AI improve home automation for energy efficiency?"
- "What are some AI applications that help with meal planning?"
- "How can AI assist in organizing daily tasks?"
- "Discuss the future of AI in smart home technology."
- "What role does AI play in enhancing personal security at home?"

Examples of Bad Prompts

Technology

- "What is AI?" (Too vague; lacks context)
- "Explain AI without using any technical terms." (Unrealistic expectation)
- "Tell me everything about AI." (Overly broad and unmanageable)
- "Is AI the best?" (Subjective without a clear focus)
- "List random AI tools." (Lacks specific direction)

Health and Wellness

- "How can AI make me healthy?" (Too general; needs specifics)
- "Tell me about AI in hospitals." (Vague; lacks depth)
- "Can AI cure diseases?" (Oversimplifies complex issues)
- "What are health apps?" (Not specific to AI)
- "Give me random health tips." (Unrelated to AI)

Education

- "What's wrong with schools?" (Negative framing; lacks context)
- "How can AI help students?" (Too broad; needs specifics)
- "Tell me about the future of education." (Vague and unfocused)
- "List AI tools for teachers." (Lacks a context for use)
- "What should I learn?" (Unclear; needs direction)

Business and Marketing

- "How can I get rich with AI?" (Unrealistic expectation)
- "Tell me about AI in marketing." (Too vague; lacks specifics)
- "What's the best AI tool?" (Subjective and lacks context)
- "How do I sell using AI?" (Too broad; needs a focused strategy)
- "Discuss business strategies." (Not specific to AI)

Creative Arts

- "Make me a song with AI." (Too broad; lacks specifics)
- "What is art?" (Philosophical and vague)
- "Explain how to create art." (Not focused on AI)
- "Can AI replace artists?" (Overly simplistic and confrontational)
- "Give me random art ideas." (Lacks direction)

Environmental Sustainability

- "How can I save the planet?" (Too general; needs specifics)
- "Tell me about pollution." (Not specific to AI)
- "What are green technologies?" (Too broad; lacks focus)
- "Discuss climate change." (Unfocused; lacks AI context)
- "How do I recycle?" (Not related to AI)

Finance

- "Make me a millionaire with AI." (Unrealistic expectation)

- "What's the best investment?" (Too vague and subjective)
- "Explain stocks." (Not specific to AI)
- "How do I manage money?" (General; lacks AI context)
- "Tell me about taxes." (Not relevant to AI)

Travel and Tourism

- "What's the best place to travel?" (Too subjective)
- "Tell me about vacations." (Lacks focus on AI)
- "How do I book a flight?" (Not related to AI)
- "Discuss travel tips." (Too broad; lacks specifics)
- "What are fun activities?" (General; no AI context)

Sports and Fitness

- "How do I become a star athlete?" (Unrealistic; lacks actionable advice)
- "What's a good workout?" (Too vague; lacks specifics)
- "Tell me about sports." (Not focused on AI)
- "How can I lose weight?" (General and lacks AI context)
- "Discuss exercise." (Too broad; needs focus on AI)

Social Issues

- "What's wrong with society?" (Negative framing; too broad)
- "Discuss poverty." (Not specific to AI)
- "How can I change the world?" (Overly broad; lacks focus)
- "Tell me about social justice." (Vague; needs context)
- "What should we do about crime?" (Too general; lacks specificity)

Entertainment

- "What's the best movie?" (Subjective; lacks context)
- "Tell me about games." (Too vague; lacks focus on AI)

- "How do I enjoy music?" (Not specific to AI)
- "What's popular now?" (Too broad and unhelpful)
- "Discuss entertainment." (General; lacks AI focus)

Home and Lifestyle

- "How do I organize my life?" (Too general; needs specifics)
- "Tell me about cleaning." (Not related to AI)
- "What's the best home?" (Subjective and vague)
- "Discuss daily routines." (Unfocused; lacks AI context)
- "How can I make my home nice?" (General; lacks specifics)

Here's a list of unique AI prompts that people commonly use:

Unique AI Prompt Examples

- "What are three health benefits of drinking green tea?"
- "Create a fun recipe using only five ingredients."
- "Summarize the plot of 'The Great Gatsby' in three sentences."
- "Generate a list of ten unique gift ideas for a birthday party."
- "Explain the concept of blockchain technology in simple terms."
- "What are five lesser-known facts about space exploration?"
- "Write a short poem about autumn."
- "Create a workout plan for beginners looking to get fit."
- "What are the major themes in Shakespeare's 'Hamlet'?"
- "Suggest three movies based on a love for science fiction."

These prompts will help you generate diverse and interesting responses from AI tools. Feel free to modify them to better suit your needs!

Chapter 6: Understanding the Importance of Data

In the world of artificial intelligence, data is often described as the lifeblood that fuels the algorithms and systems we rely on. Without high-quality data, AI models cannot function effectively, making it essential for anyone looking to dive into the field to understand data's significance. In this chapter, we'll explore why data matters, how to collect and prepare it, and the ethical considerations involved in handling data. Whether you're a beginner or a professional, grasping these concepts will empower you to harness AI effectively.

Data: The Heartbeat of AI

Why Quality Matters: The Data Dilemma

When it comes to AI, the phrase "garbage in, garbage out" holds particularly true. The quality of data directly affects the accuracy and reliability of AI models. Poor-quality data can lead to flawed predictions and decision-making, ultimately undermining the value of the AI system. Therefore, investing time in understanding and ensuring data quality is paramount.

- **Accuracy:** Data must be correct and representative of the real-world scenario it intends to model.
- **Completeness:** Missing data can lead to significant gaps in analysis,

skewing results.
- **Consistency:** Data collected from various sources should align and be formatted uniformly.

Consider an example where an AI model is trained to identify diseases from medical images. If the training data consists of poorly labeled or low-resolution images, the model's performance will suffer, potentially leading to incorrect diagnoses. Quality data not only builds trust in AI systems but also enhances their practical applications across various sectors.

Different Types of Data: A Colorful Overview

Understanding the different types of data is essential for anyone involved in AI. Data can be broadly categorized into two types: structured and unstructured.

Structured Data: This type is highly organized and easily searchable, often found in databases. Examples include spreadsheets and SQL databases. It typically adheres to a fixed schema, making it straightforward to input, query, and analyze.
Examples of Structured Data:

- **Databases:** Tables in SQL databases, such as customer information (name, email, phone number).
- **Spreadsheets:** Excel sheets with clearly defined columns for sales data (date, product, price, quantity).
- **Forms:** Online registration forms where user inputs are structured (dropdowns, text fields).

Unstructured Data: This includes any data that doesn't fit neatly into a table. Unstructured data lacks a predefined format or organization, making it more complex to analyze. It often consists of text-heavy information or multimedia.
Examples of Unstructured Data:

- **Text Documents:** Emails, articles, and reports that contain free text.
- **Multimedia Files:** Images, audio files (like podcasts), and videos.
- **Social Media Posts:** Tweets, Facebook posts, or Instagram captions that don't follow a structured format.

Both types have their significance in AI:

- Structured data is typically easier to analyze and can be processed quickly.
- Unstructured data, while more complex, often contains rich insights and can provide deeper contextual understanding.

Familiarizing yourself with these categories can help you determine which data types are most relevant for your AI projects.

Collecting and Prepping Your Data

Practical Tips for Data Collection

The next step in your data journey involves collecting data. This process can be both straightforward and challenging, depending on the type of data you need and its availability.

- **Use Open Datasets:** Platforms like Kaggle and the UCI Machine Learning Repository offer free datasets for various fields.
- **Surveys and Questionnaires:** If you require specific data, consider designing surveys to collect information directly from your target audience.
- **Web Scraping:** For more advanced users, web scraping tools can gather data from websites. Ensure you comply with the website's terms of service.

By leveraging these methods, you can build a dataset that meets your project's needs.

Cleaning It Up: Making Data Shine

Once you have gathered your data, the next crucial step is data cleaning. Raw data often comes with inconsistencies, duplicates, and errors that must be addressed before analysis.

- **Remove Duplicates:** Ensure that your dataset doesn't contain any duplicate entries that can skew results.
- **Fill in Missing Values:** Use statistical methods to estimate and fill in gaps where data is missing.
- **Standardize Formats:** Ensure that dates, numbers, and text entries follow a consistent format for ease of analysis.

By cleaning your data, you're setting the foundation for accurate and reliable AI outcomes. It's a time-consuming process, but well worth the effort for the insights you'll uncover.

Understanding AI Ethics and Bias: Your Responsibility

Ensuring Quality Data, Privacy, and Ethical Considerations

As you navigate the world of data, it's essential to consider ethical implications. Data can reflect societal biases, and if not managed correctly, AI systems can perpetuate these biases.

- **Bias in Data:** If a dataset lacks diversity, it may produce skewed results. For instance, facial recognition software trained predominantly on images of one demographic may fail to recognize individuals from other backgrounds.
- **Privacy Concerns:** Collecting personal data raises issues regarding consent and privacy. Always ensure you have permission to use any personal data, and anonymize it when possible.

Understanding these ethical considerations will help you create AI systems that are not only effective but also responsible and fair.

Navigating Regulations with Confidence

With increasing scrutiny on data use, it's crucial to stay informed about regulations surrounding data collection and AI. Familiarize yourself with laws such as GDPR (General Data Protection Regulation) in Europe and CCPA (California Consumer Privacy Act) in the U.S.

- **Know Your Rights:** Understand what data you can collect, how it should be stored, and the rights individuals have regarding their data.
- **Implement Best Practices:** Follow industry best practices for data security to protect sensitive information.

By being proactive about compliance and ethics, you can contribute to a more trustworthy AI landscape.

Summary

Understanding the importance of data in AI is crucial for anyone looking to leverage this powerful technology. From ensuring quality and comprehending different data types to collecting and cleaning data, each step is vital in building effective AI systems. Moreover, being aware of the ethical implications and regulations helps safeguard the integrity of your work. As you continue your AI journey, remember that quality data is not just a technical requirement; it's a moral responsibility that can significantly impact society. Embrace this knowledge, and you'll be well on your way to becoming a responsible AI practitioner!

Chapter 7: Empowerment for the Future

As we stand at the threshold of a new era driven by artificial intelligence, it's crucial to recognize not only the excitement but also the responsibility that comes with it. This chapter will explore the thrilling trends and innovations emerging in the AI landscape, address the challenges we face, and help you envision a future where AI serves as a powerful ally. By the end, you'll not only understand what's ahead but also how you can actively participate in shaping a responsible and innovative future.

Exciting Trends and Innovations on the Horizon

Emerging Technologies That Will Blow Your Mind

The pace of innovation in AI is accelerating rapidly, leading to groundbreaking technologies that promise to transform our daily lives. One of the most notable trends is the rise of generative AI, which can create text, images, music, and even video content based on simple prompts. This technology is not just for creative industries; it's reshaping how we approach content creation, marketing, and education.

Key Innovations:

- **Natural Language Processing (NLP):** This technology is making it easier for machines to understand and respond to human language. Think of chatbots that not only answer questions but also hold conversations like humans.

- **Computer Vision:** Advances in this field are enabling machines to interpret and understand visual information, leading to applications in security, healthcare, and even autonomous vehicles.
- **AI-Driven Robotics:** From manufacturing to healthcare, robots powered by AI are becoming more autonomous and capable, streamlining processes and enhancing efficiency.

The Future Workplace: What to Expect

As AI continues to evolve, so too will the workplace. We can anticipate a more collaborative environment where humans and machines work side by side, enhancing productivity and creativity. For instance, AI will help analyze data and generate insights, allowing professionals to make informed decisions faster than ever before.

Key Considerations:

- **Enhanced Collaboration:** Expect to see tools that facilitate teamwork between humans and AI, leading to more efficient project management and problem-solving.
- **Upskilling and Reskilling:** As certain tasks become automated, there will be a growing need for training programs to help employees adapt to new technologies and roles.

Challenges and Responsibilities Ahead

Job Displacement: Addressing Concerns

While the promise of AI is exciting, it's also important to address the challenges it poses. One of the most significant concerns is job displacement, as automation may replace certain roles, particularly in industries reliant on routine tasks. This shift can create anxiety among workers and necessitate a thoughtful approach to transition.

Key Strategies:

- **Support for Transitioning Workers:** Companies and governments need to implement retraining programs to help workers transition into new roles, focusing on skills that are less likely to be automated.
- **Emphasizing Creativity and Problem-Solving:** Roles that require human creativity, empathy, and critical thinking will continue to thrive, highlighting the need for education that fosters these skills.

Safety and Regulation: Keeping AI in Check

The rapid development of AI technologies brings with it the need for robust regulatory frameworks. Establishing guidelines to ensure the ethical use of AI is essential to prevent misuse and protect individuals' rights.

Key Measures:

- **Creating Ethical Guidelines:** Collaboration between governments, businesses, and ethicists is crucial in developing standards that prioritize transparency and accountability in AI systems.
- **Ongoing Oversight:** Implementing regular audits and evaluations of AI technologies can help identify and mitigate risks associated with their deployment.

Imagining a World with AI

Opportunities for Innovation

As we embrace AI, we open the door to countless opportunities for innovation across various fields. From healthcare advancements that improve patient outcomes to smart cities that enhance urban living, the possibilities are endless.

Key Areas for Exploration:

- **Healthcare:** AI can assist in diagnosing diseases early, personalizing treatment plans, and managing patient data more effectively.

- **Sustainability:** AI technologies can optimize resource use, reduce waste, and contribute to environmental sustainability efforts.

Our Shared Responsibility

Ultimately, the future of AI is a collective endeavor. It requires input from technologists, policymakers, and society as a whole. As users and creators of AI, we all bear responsibility for ensuring it benefits humanity and aligns with our values.

Key Takeaways:

- **Engage in Discussions:** Participate in community forums and discussions about AI's role in society to raise awareness and share insights.
- **Champion Ethical Practices:** Advocate for responsible AI development practices within your own circles, whether that's in your workplace or community.

Summary

The landscape of AI is filled with potential and challenges. By staying informed and proactive, you can become an active participant in this evolving narrative. Embrace the innovations ahead, tackle the challenges responsibly, and imagine a future where AI enhances our lives while fostering shared responsibility. Your journey into the world of AI is just beginning, and with the right mindset, it can be a transformative experience for you and society as a whole.

Chapter 8: Your AI Journey Starts Here!

As you embark on your AI journey, it's essential to lay a strong foundation that aligns with your interests and aspirations. This chapter is designed to help you set personal goals, build a supportive community, and ensure you stay current with the ever-evolving landscape of artificial intelligence. By the end, you'll have a clear action plan and resources to guide your exploration of this dynamic field.

Setting Your Personal AI Goals

Discovering Your Interests and Pathways

The first step in your AI journey is to identify what excites you about artificial intelligence. Are you drawn to its creative applications, or do you find the technical aspects more compelling? Reflecting on your interests can help you carve out a unique path in this expansive field.

Start by considering the different domains within AI, such as machine learning, natural language processing, computer vision, and robotics. Think about how these areas intersect with your passions. For instance, if you love storytelling, exploring generative AI for creative writing might resonate with you. Alternatively, if you're interested in data science, diving into machine learning could be a perfect fit.

Key Insights:

- **Self-Reflection:** Take time to list your interests and how they align with

AI applications.
- **Exploration:** Engage with introductory resources like online courses or tutorials to see what captures your attention.

Crafting Your Action Plan for Success

Once you have a clearer understanding of your interests, it's time to create an action plan that sets you on the path to success. This plan should include specific, measurable goals and timelines. For example, you might aim to complete an introductory AI course within the next month or work on a small AI project by the end of the quarter.

Incorporate both short-term and long-term objectives. Short-term goals could involve learning key concepts, while long-term aspirations might include becoming proficient in a specific AI tool or framework. Having a structured plan will help you stay motivated and focused.

Key Steps:

- **Set SMART Goals:** Ensure your goals are Specific, Measurable, Achievable, Relevant, and Time-bound.
- **Monitor Progress:** Regularly assess your progress and adjust your goals as needed to keep your journey aligned with your evolving interests.

Building Your Community and Networking

Engaging with Online Forums and Groups

A crucial aspect of your AI journey is building a supportive network. Online forums and communities offer valuable resources, including discussions, insights, and opportunities for collaboration. Platforms like Reddit, Stack Overflow, and specialized AI forums can connect you with like-minded individuals and experts in the field.

Participating actively in these communities can help you learn from others' experiences, ask questions, and share your own insights. Consider joining specific groups focused on your areas of interest, whether it's AI ethics, machine learning, or creative applications.

Key Strategies:

- **Join Relevant Communities:** Seek out groups on platforms like Facebook, LinkedIn, or Discord that align with your interests.
- **Engage Regularly:** Contribute to discussions, ask questions, and offer help to others to build meaningful connections.

Networking and Mentorship Opportunities

Networking is essential for personal and professional growth. Attend virtual and in-person events, such as AI conferences, meetups, and workshops, to expand your network. These events often provide opportunities to connect with industry professionals and thought leaders.

Mentorship can also play a vital role in your development. Finding a mentor with experience in your area of interest can provide valuable guidance and insight. Reach out to potential mentors through professional networks or by attending industry events.

Key Actions:

- **Attend Industry Events:** Look for AI-related webinars, conferences, or workshops to meet others in the field.
- **Seek Out Mentors:** Identify individuals whose work inspires you and reach out for mentorship opportunities.

Staying Ahead of the Curve

Tips for Keeping Up with Trends

The AI landscape is rapidly evolving, and staying informed about the latest developments is crucial. Subscribe to industry newsletters, follow AI thought leaders on social media, and regularly check reputable tech news sites to keep abreast of new technologies, research, and trends.

Engaging with diverse content, from podcasts to YouTube channels, can also provide unique perspectives and insights into the AI world. Make it a habit to allocate time each week for reading or watching relevant materials to ensure you're always in the loop.

Key Recommendations:

- **Curate Your News Sources:** Follow a mix of sources, including blogs, podcasts, and social media accounts dedicated to AI.
- **Join Professional Organizations:** Consider becoming a member of AI-related organizations that provide resources and updates on industry trends.

Continuous Learning

In the field of AI, continuous learning is key to staying relevant. Invest in online courses, workshops, and certifications that deepen your knowledge and skills. Platforms like Coursera, edX, and Udacity offer a variety of AI-related courses that cater to different skill levels.

Additionally, participating in hackathons or coding challenges can provide hands-on experience and help reinforce your learning. These activities not only enhance your skills but also allow you to collaborate with others and tackle real-world problems.

Key Practices:

- **Set Aside Learning Time:** Dedicate time each week for formal learning, whether through online courses or self-directed study.
- **Engage in Practical Experiences:** Seek out opportunities for hands-on projects, coding challenges, or community hackathons to apply what you've learned.

Summary

As you embark on your AI journey, remember that this path is uniquely yours. By setting personal goals, building a supportive community, and committing yourself to continuous learning, you're positioning yourself for success in this dynamic field. Embrace the opportunities and challenges ahead, and don't hesitate to reach out for support as you navigate this exciting landscape. Your journey into AI is just beginning, and the future holds endless possibilities.

Chapter 9: Learning Resources for AI Adventurers

As you embark on your journey into the world of artificial intelligence, having the right resources can make all the difference. In this chapter, we'll explore a variety of books, articles, and online courses that cater to both beginners and those looking to deepen their understanding of AI. By tapping into these valuable resources, you'll be equipped to navigate the ever-evolving landscape of AI with confidence and curiosity.

Books and Articles to Fuel Your Curiosity

Books are a treasure trove of knowledge, offering insights from experts in the field. For anyone eager to delve deeper into AI, several key texts stand out. These books cover a range of topics, from the technical aspects of AI to its societal implications, providing a well-rounded understanding of this complex subject.

Articles and Blogs

In addition to books, numerous articles and blogs offer up-to-date insights into AI trends and breakthroughs. Websites like Medium, Towards Data Science, and the AI Alignment Forum provide a wealth of information, often written by industry professionals and researchers. Articles and blogs offer timely updates and diverse perspectives.

CHAPTER 9: LEARNING RESOURCES FOR AI ADVENTURERS

Here are some recommended keywords you can use to search for books, articles, and blogs related to artificial intelligence (AI):

Keywords for Books:

- "Artificial Intelligence books"
- "Best books on machine learning"
- "Deep learning textbooks"
- "AI ethics literature"
- "Introduction to AI books"
- "AI in business books"
- "AI for beginners"
- "Machine learning algorithms books"
- "Data science reading list"
- "AI and society"

Keywords for Articles:

- "Latest research in AI"
- "AI trends 2024"
- "Impact of AI on jobs"
- "AI ethics articles"
- "How AI is transforming industries"
- "Artificial intelligence case studies"
- "AI applications in healthcare"
- "Challenges of AI technology"
- "AI safety and regulations"
- "Future of artificial intelligence"

Keywords for Blogs:

- "AI blogs to follow"
- "Machine learning blogs"

- "Data science and AI blogs"
- "Artificial intelligence thought leaders"
- "AI news and updates"
- "AI tutorials and guides"
- "Emerging AI technologies blog"
- "AI alignment and ethics blog"
- "Personal AI projects blog"
- "AI in daily life blog"

Further Reading and Exploration

If you find yourself captivated by AI, consider joining online book clubs or forums where you can discuss these texts with others. Engaging with a community can enhance your understanding and spark new ideas.

Additional Suggestions:

- Look for curated reading lists from universities or AI organizations to discover more niche topics.
- Use platforms like Goodreads to track your reading and see what others recommend.

Here are some effective keywords and phrases you can use to search for curated AI reading lists from universities or AI organizations:

Keywords for University Reading Lists:

- "AI reading list site:.edu"
- "Artificial Intelligence syllabus"
- "AI course reading materials"
- "Machine learning literature review"
- "University AI resources"
- "AI course recommended readings"

Keywords for AI Organizations:

- "Curated AI reading list"
- "Artificial Intelligence resources from [Organization Name]"
- "AI research papers list"
- "Machine learning reading recommendations"
- "AI organization publications"
- "AI knowledge base"

Keywords for Niche Topics:

- "Niche AI topics reading list"
- "Advanced AI literature"
- "Emerging trends in AI research"
- "AI ethics reading materials"
- "AI applications in [specific industry]"
- "Specialized AI research papers"

General Search Phrases:

- "Curated reading lists on Artificial Intelligence"
- "Best AI books and articles from universities"
- "Top AI research papers recommended by experts"
- "AI organization curated resources"
- "AI literature for advanced learners"

Online Courses: Your AI Academy

Platforms for Learning and Networking

With the rapid advancement of AI technologies, online courses have become a vital resource for learners of all levels. Various platforms offer a wide range of courses that cater to different aspects of AI, from programming to ethics.

Here's a look at some current top platforms (in no particular order) where you can find structured learning experiences:

Coursera

Coursera partners with universities and organizations offer courses in AI, machine learning, and data science. You can find beginner-friendly courses like "AI For Everyone" by Andrew Ng, which provides a non-technical introduction to AI concepts.

edX

Similar to Coursera, edX provides access to a variety of courses from institutions like Harvard and MIT. Courses such as "Introduction to Artificial Intelligence" offer foundational knowledge and practical applications.

Udacity

Udacity focuses on tech skills and offers nanodegree programs in AI and machine learning. Their "AI Programming with Python" course is excellent for those looking to gain hands-on coding experience.

Kaggle

While primarily known as a platform for data science competitions, Kaggle also offers free courses that focus on practical skills in machine learning and data analysis. It's an excellent place to learn by doing.

LinkedIn Learning

For those interested in professional development, LinkedIn Learning offers courses on AI tools, techniques, and industry applications. These can be beneficial for individuals looking to enhance their skills for career advancement.

CHAPTER 9: LEARNING RESOURCES FOR AI ADVENTURERS

Building a Network Through Online Learning

Engaging with peers and instructors in online courses can significantly enhance your learning experience. Participate in discussion forums, join study groups, and seek out mentorship opportunities to deepen your understanding of AI. Networking can also lead to collaborative projects and potential career paths.

Additional Tips:

- Set specific learning goals for each course to maintain focus.
- Consider following AI experts on social media platforms to stay informed about new courses and trends.

Keywords for Discussion Forums:

- "AI discussion forums"
- "Artificial Intelligence community"
- "Machine learning forums"
- "AI chat groups"
- "Data science forums"
- "AI Reddit communities"
- "AI enthusiast groups"
- "Online AI discussions"

Keywords for Study Groups:

- "AI study groups"
- "Machine learning study sessions"
- "AI book clubs"
- "Data science study groups"
- "Online learning cohorts for AI"
- "AI project collaboration groups"
- "AI learning circles"

Keywords for Mentorship Opportunities:

- "AI mentorship programs"
- "Find an AI mentor"
- "AI mentorship network"
- "Artificial Intelligence career guidance"
- "Data science mentorship"
- "AI professional networking"
- "AI career coaching"

General Search Phrases:

- "Join AI forums for beginners"
- "Online communities for AI learners"
- "Study groups for AI enthusiasts"
- "AI mentorship opportunities online"
- "Collaborate on AI projects"

Using these keywords in search engines, social media platforms, or specific sites like LinkedIn, Reddit, or GitHub can help you find relevant groups and opportunities to enhance your AI learning experience.

Summary

As you venture into the world of AI, remember that continuous learning is essential. With a variety of books and online courses at your fingertips, you have the tools to explore this fascinating field further. By immersing yourself in these resources and engaging with a community of learners, you'll not only deepen your knowledge but also position yourself as an informed participant in the ongoing dialogue about AI's role in our lives. Embrace this journey with curiosity and enthusiasm, and watch as your understanding of AI unfolds!

Conclusion: Embrace Your AI Future!

As we reach the end of this journey through the realm of artificial intelligence, it's time to reflect on what you've learned and how you can apply that knowledge in your daily life and future endeavors. AI is not just a buzzword; it's a powerful tool that can enhance your experiences, solve problems, and unlock new opportunities. This conclusion will recap the key takeaways, provide encouragement for ongoing exploration, and offer final thoughts on the significance of AI in our lives.

Recap of Key Takeaways

Celebrating Your Knowledge Gains

Throughout this book, you've gained a foundational understanding of AI, its applications, and the responsibilities that come with using this technology. You've explored everything from the basics of algorithms and data to the exciting trends on the horizon. It's essential to celebrate these milestones in your learning journey.

Take a moment to reflect on the topics that resonated with you the most. Perhaps it was the creative applications of AI in personal projects or the ethical considerations surrounding its use. Recognizing your growth will not only reinforce your learning but also motivate you to continue exploring the field.

Key Takeaways:

- **Foundational Knowledge:** You now understand core AI concepts and their

applications.
- **Recognition of Growth:** Reflect on what you've learned to reinforce your knowledge and motivation.

The Importance of Ethical AI Use

As you become more familiar with AI, it's crucial to remember the ethical implications of its use. Responsible AI is not just about technical proficiency; it involves understanding the impact of your decisions on individuals and society. This includes being aware of issues such as data privacy, bias, and transparency.

By approaching AI with a sense of responsibility, you can contribute to its positive evolution. Ethical AI use fosters trust and enhances the benefits of technology for everyone, ensuring that innovations are inclusive and equitable.

Key Points:

- **Ethical Responsibility:** Understand the importance of using AI ethically and responsibly.
- **Positive Impact:** Strive to create inclusive and fair applications of AI technology.

Words of Encouragement for Ongoing Exploration

Keep Exploring and Innovating

The world of AI is evolving, and your journey is just beginning. Keep an open mind and continue exploring new tools, technologies, and methodologies. Whether it's participating in online courses, engaging in community projects, or experimenting with your own ideas, there are countless opportunities to expand your knowledge and skills.

Embrace the spirit of innovation. Don't be afraid to push boundaries and experiment with AI applications that excite you. Every attempt, whether successful or not, is a step toward deeper understanding and expertise.

- **Continuous Learning:** Embrace a mindset of lifelong learning and exploration.
- **Innovative Spirit:** Push the boundaries of your creativity and curiosity.

Your Role in Shaping the Future of AI

As an individual equipped with knowledge and skills in AI, you have the power to shape its future. Whether you aspire to work in technology, healthcare, education, or any other field, your insights and creativity can drive meaningful change. Remember that every contribution, no matter how small, can impact the larger conversation around AI and its applications.

Be an advocate for responsible AI practices and encourage others to join you in this journey. Your voice matters in discussions about the ethical use of AI and how it can enhance our lives.

Key Messages:

- **Active Participation:** Engage in the AI community and advocate for ethical practices.
- **Influence and Impact:** Recognize your potential to shape the future of AI through your actions.

Final Thoughts: AI and You

Embracing Technology in Daily Life

AI is woven into the fabric of our everyday lives, from smart assistants to recommendation algorithms. By embracing this technology, you can enhance your personal and professional experiences. Learn to leverage AI tools to improve productivity, foster creativity, and make informed decisions.

Remember that AI is not a replacement for human intuition and creativity; rather, it serves as a powerful partner that amplifies your abilities. Explore how you can incorporate AI into your daily routines to simplify tasks and unlock new potential.

Final Reflections:

- **Everyday Integration:** Look for ways to integrate AI into your daily life for enhanced experiences.
- **Collaboration with AI:** View AI as a partner that complements your skills and creativity.

Making a Positive Impact with AI

Your journey with AI is an opportunity to make a positive impact in various domains, from social issues to environmental challenges. Consider how your skills and insights can be applied to address pressing problems in society. Whether it's developing an app that supports mental health, creating solutions for energy efficiency, or advancing educational tools, the possibilities are endless.

As you move forward, keep in mind the potential of AI to drive social good. Your contributions can help ensure that technology serves humanity and fosters a brighter, more equitable future.

Final Thoughts:

- **Social Responsibility:** Leverage AI to address societal challenges and promote positive change.
- **Future Aspirations:** Think about how your journey can lead to impactful innovations in the world.

In conclusion, as you close this chapter and step into your AI future, embrace the journey ahead with curiosity and enthusiasm. The knowledge you've gained equips you to navigate the complexities of AI and harness its power for good. Celebrate your progress, continue learning, and remember that you have the ability to shape the future of this transformative technology. Your adventure with AI starts now!

Help Us Spread the Word!

Hello, Wonderful Readers!

Thank you for choosing our book! We hope it has inspired and engaged you. If you enjoyed it, we would be grateful if you could take a moment to leave a review.

Your feedback can guide others in their reading choices and help us grow. Share what you loved, any insights you gained, or suggestions for improvement—every bit of your experience counts!

To leave a review, just visit the platform where you bought the book, click "Write a Review," and share your thoughts. Your voice matters, and we appreciate your support!

Thank you for being part of our journey!

Warmly,
S K Hampshire

GLOSSARY OF TERMS

- **AI-Driven Fitness Trackers**: Devices monitoring activity and providing health insights.
- **AI-Driven Robotics**: Robotics enhanced by AI for autonomy and efficiency.
- **AI Ethics**: Considerations regarding the moral implications of AI, including data bias and privacy concerns.
- **AI Model**: Mathematical representation of a process created through data training.
- **AI-Powered Automation**: Using AI to automate processes, enhancing efficiency and productivity.
- **Algorithms**: Sets of rules for solving problems or making decisions based on data.
- **Artificial Intelligence (AI)**: Simulation of human intelligence in machines to perform tasks requiring cognitive functions.
- **Automate**: Using technology to perform tasks without human intervention.
- **Backpropagation**: A training process adjusting weights based on prediction errors.
- **Bias in AI**: Systematic errors from prejudiced assumptions in the ML process, affecting fairness.
- **Big Data Analytics**: Examining large data sets to uncover patterns and insights.
- **Cognitive Behavioral Therapy (CBT) Tools**: Digital resources for managing mental health.
- **Cognitive Functions**: Mental processes related to thinking and learning.

- **Collective Responsibility**: Shared obligation to ensure AI benefits humanity.
- **Community Engagement**: Raising awareness about AI's societal impact.
- **Computer Vision**: AI interpreting visual information.
- **Continuous Learning**: Ongoing pursuit of knowledge to stay relevant in AI.
- **Cross-Validation**: Method estimating model skill by dividing data into training and testing subsets.
- **Curate Your News Sources**: Selecting diverse sources to stay informed about AI trends.
- **Data**: The essential information used to train AI models; often described as the "lifeblood" of AI.
- **Data Analytics**: Examining datasets to extract meaningful insights.
- **Data Augmentation**: Techniques to expand training datasets artificially.
- **Data Cleaning**: Preparing raw data for analysis by addressing inconsistencies and errors.
- **Data Collection Methods**: Techniques for gathering data, including surveys and web scraping.
- **Data Quality**: The accuracy, completeness, and consistency of data, affecting AI model performance.
- **Deep Learning**: A subset of machine learning using neural networks with multiple layers.
- **Dropout**: A regularization technique preventing overfitting during training.
- **Echoing**: Referring to related concepts within the text to reinforce understanding.
- **Engagement**: Active participation to enhance understanding and retention.
- **Explainable AI (XAI)**: AI systems providing understandable explanations for their decisions.
- **Ethical Guidelines**: Standards ensuring responsible AI use.
- **Ethical Implications**: Moral considerations regarding the impacts of AI technologies.

- **Feature Engineering**: Selecting or creating new features from raw data to enhance model performance.
- **Feature Extraction**: Transforming raw data into characteristics usable for ML models.
- **Feedback Mechanism**: Provides information on the success of actions in reinforcement learning.
- **Generative Adversarial Networks (GANs)**: Frameworks where two neural networks compete to generate new data.
- **Generative AI**: AI that creates new content based on prompts.
- **Human-in-the-Loop (HITL)**: Model design integrating human feedback into ML processes.
- **Image Classification**: A machine learning task categorizing images into predefined classes.
- **Image Style Transfer**: Applying the artistic style of one image to another using neural networks.
- **Inference**: Using a trained model to make predictions on unseen data.
- **Information Retrieval**: AI's ability to quickly access data.
- **Iteration**: The process of repeatedly refining a project based on testing and feedback.
- **Job Displacement**: Concern about automation replacing certain jobs.
- **Kaggle Datasets**: A platform offering a vast collection of datasets for data science projects.
- **Machine Learning (ML)**: A subset of AI allowing systems to learn from data patterns.
- **Mental Health Apps**: Applications offering personalized mental health support.
- **Mentorship**: Guidance from experienced individuals in AI.
- **Natural Language Generation (NLG)**: NLP subfield generating human-like text from structured data.
- **Natural Language Processing (NLP)**: AI enabling understanding and responding to human language.
- **Neural Networks**: Computational models inspired by the human brain for recognizing patterns.

- **Ongoing Oversight**: Regular auditing of AI systems to identify risks.
- **Overfitting**: A modeling error where a model learns training data too well.
- **Personalized Experiences**: Tailored online interactions based on user preferences.
- **Personalized Recommendations**: Creating systems that suggest items based on user preferences.
- **Predictive Analytics**: Using historical data to forecast future trends.
- **Productivity Apps**: Software tools enhanced by AI to improve workflows.
- **Productivity Tools**: AI applications that automate routine tasks to enhance efficiency.
- **Reinforcement** Learning: Learning through interaction and feedback in an environment.
- **Regularization**: Technique preventing overfitting by penalizing complexity.
- **Segmentation Analysis**: Dividing customers into groups for tailored marketing.
- **Sentiment Analysis**: Analyzing text data to determine its emotional tone.
- **Smart Assistants**: AI devices (e.g., Siri, Alexa) that perform tasks via voice commands.
- **Structured Data**: Highly organized data that is easily searchable.
- **Sustainability in AI**: Optimizing resource use and reducing waste with AI.
- **Task Management**: Organizing and prioritizing tasks, often aided by AI.
- **Teachable Machine**: A web-based tool for creating simple machine learning models.
- **Transfer Function**: Describes the input-output relationship of a system.
- **Transfer Learning**: Adapting a pre-trained model to a new, related task.
- **Underfitting**: Scenario where a model is too simple, capturing no underlying data patterns.
- **Upskilling and Reskilling**: Training workers to adapt to new technologies.
- **Voice Assistant**: Developing an AI application that recognizes and responds to voice commands.
- **Wearable Devices**: Technology worn on the body that tracks health metrics.

References

References

Bostrom, N. (2014). *Superintelligence: Paths, dangers, strategies.* Oxford University Press.

Domingos, P. (2015). *The master algorithm: How the quest for the ultimate learning machine will remake our world.* Basic Books.

Goertzel, K., & Pennachin, C. (2007). *Artificial general intelligence.* Springer.

Goodfellow, I., Bengio, Y., & Courville, A. (2016). *Deep learning.* MIT Press.

Jordan, M. I., & Mitchell, T. M. (2015). Machine learning: Trends, perspectives, and prospects. *Science, 349*(6245), 255-260. https://doi.org/10.1126/science.aaa8415

Kumar, A., & Gupta, R. (2020). Role of artificial intelligence in healthcare: A review. *Journal of Healthcare Engineering, 2020,* 1-12. https://doi.org/10.1155/2020/8871028

Marr, B. (2018). *Artificial intelligence in practice: How 50 successful companies used AI and machine learning to solve problems.* Wiley.

Marr, B. (2018). *Data strategy: How to profit from a world of big data, analytics and the Internet of Things.* Kogan Page Publishers.

REFERENCES

Manning, C. D., Raghavan, P., & Schütze, H. (2008). *Introduction to information retrieval*. MIT Press.

Russell, S., & Norvig, P. (2020). *Artificial intelligence: A modern approach* (4th ed.). Pearson.

Silver, D., Sutton, R. S., & Müller, M. (2016). Reinforcement learning: A survey. *Journal of Machine Learning Research, 16*, 213-221.

Online Resources

1. Chatbot.com. (n.d.). Create your chatbot in minutes. Retrieved from https://www.chatbot.com/
2. Coursera. (n.d.). Online courses in artificial intelligence. Retrieved from https://www.coursera.org
3. Data.gov. (n.d.). The U.S. Government's open data. Retrieved from https://www.data.gov/
4. edX. (n.d.). AI programs and courses. Retrieved from https://www.edx.org
5. FiveThirtyEight. (n.d.). Datasets. Retrieved from https://data.fivethirtyeight.com
6. Google. (n.d.). Teachable machine. Retrieved from https://teachablemachine.withgoogle.com
7. Google. (n.d.). Dataset search. Retrieved from https://datasetsearch.research.google.com
8. IBM. (n.d.). Watson Studio. Retrieved from https://www.ibm.com/cloud/watson-studio
9. Kaggle. (n.d.). Datasets: A collection of data for data science. Retrieved from https://www.kaggle.com/datasets
10. Lobe. (n.d.). A free, easy-to-use tool for building machine learning models. Retrieved from https://www.lobe.ai/
11. Microsoft. (n.d.). Azure Machine Learning Studio. Retrieved from https://azure.microsoft.com/en-us/services/machine-learning/

12. OpenAI. (n.d.). The potential and impact of generative AI. Retrieved from https://openai.com
13. Reddit. (n.d.). AI communities on Reddit. Retrieved from https://www.reddit.com
14. Runway. (n.d.). Runway ML: A creative toolkit for machine learning. Retrieved from https://runwayml.com/
15. UCI Machine Learning Repository. (n.d.). Datasets. Retrieved from https://archive.ics.uci.edu/ml/index.php
16. World Health Organization. (n.d.). Global Health Observatory Data. Retrieved from https://www.who.int/data/gho